A Nickel A Ride

A FOLK HISTORY OF PORT DALHOUSIE DURING THE PAST CENTURY

Christine Robertson & David Serafino

DALPEER PRODUCTIONS

A NICKEL A RIDE

Published by:
Dalpeer
6 Pine Street
St. Catharines Ontario Canada L2N 4T1
Ph. (905) 934-9777 Fax (905) 934-0667
E-mail: dalpeer@niagara.net

CANADIAN CATALOGUING
IN PUBLICATION DATA

Robertson, Christine, 1949-
    A nickel a ride: a folk history of Port Dalhousie during the past century

ISBN 0-9685401-0-4

1. Port Dalhousie (St. Catharines, Ont.) - History. I. Serafino, David,
1947- . II. Title.

FC3099.S23Z5 1999   971.3'38   C99-931359-2
F1059.5.S14R62 1999

Printed at Skyway Reprographics, St. Catharines, Ontario, Canada

FOREWORD

here are those who remember the days when a nickel could buy a streetcar trip to Port Dalhousie, a ride on the carousel, or a ticket for a dance. But even if one didn't have a nickel, then the beach and the water were still free.

During the past century, both prices and water levels have risen. The beach is narrower and the midway and dancehall are long gone. However, much in town has survived—some in the form of restoration and the rest in the memories of those who lived their lives here in this bustling harbour community.

History has a richness when told first-hand. For the most part, the people who tell their stories in this book are octogenarians. The topics run through the era of the fishing industry, the days of prohibition, and a half-century of steamers and fun in Lakeside Park. Many talk of early memories as children growing up in the village and some recall even older stories related by parents. Most of our narrators are still living here with us today, yet others, those who were interviewed more than twenty years ago, have since passed away. We are indebted to them all for their honest words which we are only too eager to share.

As Port Dalhousie enters a new century, we can look back over the past 100 years to see how life has changed. Through the eyes of others we can recognize values that survive the times. We can also assess what has been lost, what has been saved, what has been gained and what is yet to be achieved. We can celebrate a quality of life which can be held up as an ideal.

From the harbour through the bustling core, along a world-class rowing course and onto tree-lined streets, a proudly unique heritage emanates. Both resident and visitor can still enjoy a stroll along the pier, a day at the beach or a trek around the harbour, but now in greater comfort and safety. Each step in any direction offers a scenic vista filled with the quiet of nature's tranquility or with the sounds of people having fun.

Granted, it now costs two-dollars to catch a downtown bus to Port Dalhousie, but the carousel is still a nickel a ride and, most importantly, the best is still free. ¤

CONTENTS

— INTRODUCTION —

ALMOST AN ISLAND

The beauty of the old town is in its blend of positive and negative space. Comparable to the work of an artist, a balance is struck between the image itself and that which surrounds it. Almost an island, *Port Dalhousie* today boasts a picturesque harbour, a world class rowing course, a popular beachfront, and an extensive shoreline. Surrounded by so much water, it is only natural that recreational activities abound. Sailing, rowing, fishing, swimming, jet-skiing, beach volleyball—the list seems to increase with every passing summer season. With winter comes a welcome solitude. The frozen surf by the pier offers just one of many photographic opportunities. *Martindale Pond* becomes a skating rink. Cross-country skiers readily access *Henley Island*, cross over to the evocative *Green Ribbon Trail* and venture up the length of *Richardson's Creek*.

In recent years Port Dalhousie has become a popular tourist destination and a favoured place to live. Along with restaurants, boutiques and recreational opportunities, there remains a strong dedication to a sense of community. Though the look of the village has changed dramatically through the century, as has its economic focus, the bonds within the neighbourhood remain strong. In spite of having lost the right to call itself a town when incorporated into the *City of St. Catharines* in 1960, an identity is maintained as something separate and unique.

Port Dalhousie is what it is today because of the people who live here. Some arrived as adults and fell in love with the town. Others were born and raised here, and several can trace their families back to somewhere near the beginning. In the early 1800s this artificial harbour developed as the original terminus of the *First Welland Canal*. The village became a town evolving through various stages of prosperity and decline. The greatest and most recent decline happened in 1932 when the *Fourth Welland Canal* was opened and the Lake Ontario Terminal moved three miles east to *Port Weller*. Though Port Dalhousie continued on as an industrial centre and enjoyed several decades as a recreational destination, it eventually faded into oblivion.

Renewal began in 1974 when Government monies were made available through the *Neigbourhood Improvement Program* (N.I.P.) to resurrect this healthy yet, for a short time, neglected community.

BENIGN NEGLECT

In 1974, most of the commercial buildings were vacant and crumbling. In other parts of the city, development was gobbling up prime agricultural land for subdivisions while historic buildings were being replaced with office towers. The commercial core of Port Dalhousie survived. It was a benign neglect that saved it, yet it was the community itself that resurrected it.

A prerequisite of being granted a N.I.P. grant was that a quorum of 50 people from within the neighbourhood had to be developed to champion the cause. *Rennie Park* is named after **James Rennie** who was extremely active door-to-door and in meetings to move the project forward. Unfortunately, Mr. Rennie passed away before he could witness the fruits of his labours; however, he was a significant individual responsible for setting the wheels in motion—wheels which began to move faster and with more momentum as time moved on. His friends fought to have the new park named after him in recognition of his dedication to resurrecting the town that he loved.

Although renovations in some buildings began earlier and took place sporadically, the demarcation point for "Port's new beginning" is fixed at the restoration of the *Murphy Building* at the corner of *Lock Street* and *Lakeport Road* (formerly Front Street). The significance of this undertaking was that the new owners, **Blake and Lillian Harley**, recognized the value of historical restoration. Developing this "cornerstone" building to house several retail shops and a restaurant, paved the way for similar restorations.

In 1979 when *Murphy's Restaurant* opened in the main floor of the building, it joined the long established *Marie's Seafood Restaurant*, the *Lion Tavern*, *the Lakeside Hotel* and the *Port Hotel* as one of Port Dalhousie's licensed establishments. Today there are at least fourteen—nowhere near the number that once existed when the town made its trade from passing ships and their thirsty crews.

The times have certainly changed. One can only imagine wooden sailing ships being pulled into the canal lock by a team of horses, or when families of fishermen lived on the beach. Many do recall the days when ferry boats carried passengers daily between Toronto and Port Dalhousie and the streetcars which brought crowds of people to enjoy the beach and the midway with its dancehall and carnival rides.

These were fun-filled times as well as being days of industry and the work whistle. Always a working man's town, the unique character seems to have developed from a sensible balance of work and play. Though little has been written about the town and those who made this spit of land their home, there are some who have made the effort to share their memories with you. Now, having spent your nickel, you are invited to enjoy the ride. ¤

Part I

A BRIEF HISTORY OF PORT DALHOUSIE

A legendary character paddles in front of a legendary beach

THE EARLY SETTLERS

Before the Europeans arrived, the land on the Lake Ontario shore at the mouth of *Twelve Mile Creek* was inhabited by indigenous people. Comprised of marsh and dense forest it provided an abundant supply of fish and game. The *Neutral Indians* built their villages in the coastal areas and hunted in the interior wilderness clearing forests and creating trails. This would prove advantageous to the French settlers who followed. One such Indian trail eventually later developed into what is now *Martindale Road*.

In 1650, the Neutral Indians were annihilated by the *Iroquois*. Soon after, the *Mississaugas*, a branch of the *Chippawa Tribe*, settled in this area and further developed trails that would be used by the French.

French explorers who were looking for a route between Lake Erie and Lake Ontario, other than the treacherous Niagara River, made the first maps of the Niagara Peninsula. Not only were they searching for sites close to lakes for water transportation, creeks for operating their mills, but also for sandy soil that could be easily cleared of its trees.

At the time of the American Revolutionary War of 1775, the Thirteen Colonies consisted of approximately three million people. Of these, it is believed that one million were Loyalists who opposed the war and chose to remain faithful to Britain. When fighting broke out, the British Government formed regiments of colonial soldiers from among the Loyalists. Some fought with *Butler's Rangers*. During the period between the British evacuating Boston in 1776, and the signing of the Treaty of Versailles in 1783, many Loyalists fled north to avoid further persecution after having their lands confiscated. It was clear that the British government would have to compensate the Loyalists.

When the war ended and Butler's Rangers disbanded, these Loyalists received Crown grants as well as tools, clothing, seeds, food and livestock. Their rank and status determined the size, location and quality of the grants. The new settlers did not begin on equal footing.

The R.F. Foote House, also known as 'The Breakers'

At the top of the hierarchy were the Loyalist officers and the Scottish merchants. They became the leaders of the community. All this did not come without a price. The land was granted on a temporary basis. In order to keep their land, the settlers had a specific amount of time to clear it and make it self-supporting. Initially they lived in tents, then cabins in the forest and later formed village communities. By axe, they cleared trees for their cabins that were seldom more than two rooms. The roofs were made of bark or split logs, blankets often served as doors, and windows were covered with oiled waxed paper. Furniture was made by hand, and in some cases, the flat stump of a tree served as the family dinner table. Stone fireplaces were used for cooking and heating.

They planted potatoes, turnips and corn by hoe and spade. They sowed wheat seeds by hand and blanketed them with tree limbs to keep away the hungry birds. Before the flour and gristmills were built, the grain was separated from the stock by flailing, and the wheat was pounded between rocks or in a hollow hardwood stump with a pestle. They worked from daylight to dark and barely had enough food to feed their families. Many had no food left though their harvest was three months away. In the autumn of 1787 there was a crop failure and in 1788 the settlers faced famine. From the Indians they learned the medicinal and food value of roots, herbs and greens. Many wore clothes made of deerskin and soon began growing flax. By noticing what the pigs ate, they avoided anything poisonous and, those fortunate enough to have cows, lived on milk.

One of the first United Empire Loyalist settlers *was **Captain Peter Tenbroeck***, an officer in Butler's Rangers. In 1796 he received over eight hundred acres of Crown land. ***Benjamin Pawling***, also a Butler's Ranger, received a large tract of land in the township of *Grantham* just east of Port Dalhousie. He and his brother *Jesse Pawling* were sons of a Welshman who settled in Pennsylvania before the American Revolutionary War. Later Jesse married Captain Tenbroeck's daughter, *Gertrude*, and they had several children. On December 28, 1821, Captain Tenbroeck's son *Jacob* sold to *Henry Pawling* (Jesse and Gertrude's son) 300 acres of land now in Port Dalhousie. On the same day, Henry deeded the land to his younger brother **Nathan Pawling** who became a prominent and active member of the community. He performed the duties of magistrate, postmaster, schoolteacher, storekeeper, as well as operating a farm along the Twelve Mile Creek.

In 1821 the settlement was named '*Dalhousie*' after the **Earl of Dalhousie** who was *Governor General of Canada* from

On the beach below The Breakers

1820 to 1828. Nathan respected the Earl and had followed his career. Both men shared the idea of developing a canal between Lake Erie and Lake Ontario. Many felt the town should be named after Nathan Pawling, but Pawling felt otherwise.

On April 5, 1826 Squire Pawling placed an advertisement in the *Farmer's Journal and Welland Canal Intelligencer* in an attempt to encourage new settlers to the area. He presented an enticing picture of life in the small settlement. Mention was also made of the soon to be completed canal and all its advantages. Despite his depiction, those who arrived faced the same hardships as their predecessors in their attempts to clear and cultivate the land, build homes for their families and establish businesses.

The eventual development of Port Dalhousie was a result of the decision to locate the northern terminus of the First Welland Canal here—a decision avidly sought by **William Hamilton Merritt** and other mill owners who were in search of a steady and abundant source of water. In 1829 the opening of the First Welland Canal began a new era in Port Dalhousie's history. ¤

First Welland Canal
1824

On a frosty morning of November 27, 1829 the British schooner '*Ann & Jane*', was the first vessel to enter Lock One in Port Dalhousie. Followed closely by *R. H. Boughton* of Youngstown, N.Y., the two ships slowly began the historic ascent of the locks to *Port Robinson*. Colours were streaming from all parts of their rigging and the 'Ann & Jane' carried a silk flag with the words '*The King, God Bless Him*' imprinted in gold letters. Once in Port Robinson, they passed into the *Welland River* and moved eastward to *Chippawa* up the *Niagara River* to arrive in *Buffalo* on December 2.

As it was so late in the season, the ice in some parts of the canal was two to three inches thick. In order to allow the passage of the schooners, the ice had to be broken up by a scow. The inclement weather did not deter the great numbers of people who crowded the banks firing muskets and hailing the vessels as they gracefully made their way through each lock.

The following is an eyewitness account (*Farmers' Journal and Welland Canal Intelligencer, Dec. , 1829*) of the opening of navigation between Lake Ontario and Lake Erie:

"*Ann & Jane of York and R. H. Boughton of Youngstown decorated with flags, ensigns, pendants and, in a fanciful style, effected their passage through this village and all the locks above on the Welland Canal with ease and safety, amid the spontaneous and hearty cheers and salutes of those assembled to witness the exhilarating scene.*"

This marked the beginning of an era of transportation and commerce that would bring prosperity and rapid growth to the settlement.

The idea of this waterway was born as early as 1710 when Louis XIV's engineer, *De la Mothe*, believed that a canal could be built to bypass the cataracts of Niagara. Also, *Robert Hamilton*, over a decade before his death in 1809, conceived the idea of a waterway around Niagara Falls. But, it wasn't until *William Hamilton Merritt* became

The 'Lakeside' landing   *c.1900*

interested in the prospects of an inland channel that real progress began.

In 1796, when Merritt was three, his family, United Empire Loyalists, brought him to the area near the Twelve Mile Creek. He fought in the War of 1812 and upon his return purchased land on the banks of the Twelve. In 1816, he began operating a sawmill and soon owned several mills and was in need of a steady and ample supply of water to maintain his operations effectively. Initially he intended to convey water from the Welland River to his mills, which were often idle. The idea of a channel connecting the lakes developed later.

So, in the fall of the year, with the aid of two fellow mill owners, *John De Cew* and *George Keefer*, and a borrowed water level, Merritt conducted the first surveys for the water route. He believed that a feeder canal could be cut from the headwaters of the Twelve Mile Creek through the Short Hills of Pelham to Chippawa Creek. As his businesses were suffering, he was personally unable to finance the construction and thus developed the idea of a commercial waterway carrying ships of trade.

Another element also served to generate interest in the peninsular waterway. As work on the *Erie Canal* (1817-1825) had commenced the year before, it was believed (and rightly so) that unless an internal seaway was developed, much of the upper lake traffic would be diverted to New York via the Hudson River.

On June 19, 1824, the Government of Upper Canada granted a charter to the *Welland Canal Company*, a private enterprise. After several surveys were conducted and amendments to proposed plans and actual routes made, stage one of the First Welland Canal was completed. Merritt and other mill owners on the Creek were now provided with a regular supply of water to ensure continual operation and success of their mills.

The entrance to the canal was at the west end of Lakeside Park. The route passed along the northeast side of Lock Street, behind the present Lincoln Fabrics and then followed the natural course of the Twelve Mile Creek to Merritton. It then moved on to Port Robinson, along the Welland River to Chippawa and up the Niagara River to Lake Erie.

The year was 1829, and the canal was now ready to receive the numerous sail craft which would ply the waters and ornament the landscape of Niagara in the years ahead. ¤

1922 aerial view of the inner harbour. Left to right: 1st lock of the 3rd Welland Canal; Spillway, Maple Leaf Rubber Company, 1st lock of the 2nd Welland Canal, Muir Brothers Dry Docks.

Early Growth

W hen the First Welland Canal was completed, Port Dalhousie was just a small settlement. As the canal traffic increased, canal related industries developed, attracting millers and labourers. This migration to the area also fuelled a demand for industry and services to meet the needs of the growing settlement.

Shipbuilding became a major industry. In 1837, **Robert Abbey**, a Scotsman whose trade was boat building, established a shipyard at Port Dalhousie, building yawls, sailing yachts and steam yachts. In the same year, another Scottish immigrant, **Alexander Muir,** arrived.

Muir had originally left Scotland, to take a position on board a sailing vessel, making several trips here and to China and India. On a return trip to Port Dalhousie, he bought ten acres of land on Queen Street (now Dalhousie Avenue) for sixty dollars and built a house on it, though he did not immediately settle there.

After several more years sailing, and having observed the need for facilities to repair vessels, Muir, along with his four brothers, began constructing their dry dock in 1850. Built on the east side of the canal, it was subsequently launched and towed to the north of the canal at the site later occupied by the permanent dry dock. It was the birth of an enterprise that provided numerous jobs and was largely responsible for the growth of Port Dalhousie.

Shortly after the first canal was completed, it became evident that it was inefficient and could not accommodate the volume of traffic. Through the years, as traffic increased and larger ships were being built, the channel proved too narrow and shallow. In 1841, after the union of Upper and Lower Canada, the government purchased the entire company from the private stockholders and began the much needed canal revisions. In 1842, construction on the *Second Welland Canal* began.

1842 was also the year that the first steam vessel traveled through, the consequences of which were suffered by the tow-teams. Prior to steam powered ships, towing of boats was an important factor of canal

Lock One, Third Welland Canal   c.1900

navigation. As the barges, sloops, scows and schooners had no power
with which to propel themselves, they relied heavily on this service.
There were, at the time, one hundred and fifty teams of horses stabled
at the west end of what is now Lakeside Park. With the advent of
steamships and tugs for towing purposes, the use of horse and oxen
teams at Port Dalhousie and other points along the canal was on the
wane.

Mrs. Rhoda Abel recalls:

*"My brother Clyde drove one of those teams belonging to Mr. E.
McMahon. He had teams which towed the barges up. Great big heavy
teams of horses which pulled those barges to Thorold. When they got
them to the long level at Thorold, they were towed by tugs. Steamboats
were towing the barges but they couldn't fit into the lock together. The
steamboats would go through and leave the barges to be towed
through by the horse teams."*

In 1863, Port Dalhousie, with a population of 1,364, was
incorporated as a village. With Confederation in 1867, the canal was
transferred from provincial to federal jurisdiction, and the government
was soon compelled to make essential revisions and improvements. In
1869, the east pier was rebuilt and the following year, the harbour was
dredged and deepened. Work began on the *Third Welland Canal* in
1875 ushering in an era of unparalleled prosperity. A more direct

route was followed, no longer utilizing the Twelve-Mile Creek. A towpath was constructed and, although most of the vessels passed through the canal on their own power, the tow teams did remain active towing barges and sailcraft.

Continuous cross-lake ferry service was established in 1884 with the paddle-wheelers *Empress of India* and, later, the *Garden City*. In 1890, the *Austin House* (Lakeside Hotel) and the *Wellington Hotel* (Lion Tavern) were built. The same year, the *Maple Leaf Rubber Company* took over the *Lawrie Flour Mill* and built a generating facility to provide electricity to the town.

At the turn of the century, the *Muir Dry Docks* was the major employer in the village. In the years that followed, Port Dalhousie began to establish itself not only as an industrial centre but also as a recreational destination. In 1901, the *N.S.&T Railway (Niagara, St. Catharines & Toronto)* completed an electric line to Port Dalhousie on the west side of the harbour to connect with steamers from Toronto. Lakeside Park, with its extensive beach, began to develop and eventually grew to include change houses, concession booths and a merry-go-round.

Competitive rowing had become popular in Canada starting in the 1860s and, in 1903, the former Welland Canal route on Martindale Pond, protected by the high banks, was chosen as the permanent site for the Royal Canadian Henley Regatta. In 1904, a grandstand was constructed at the point overlooking the finish line and a clubhouse was built at the southern end of the course. ¤

Part II

RECOLLECTIONS

Fun at the beach   c.1905

Cutting block ice on the pond   c.1920

THE PEOPLE WHO TELL THE STORIES
A Brief Introduction

Colin Johnston Sr.

Mr. Johnston was born on February 28, 1920. He and his wife Gloria both grew up in Port Dalhousie and have been active in many aspects of the community including rowing, sailing, church and business. The Johnston family has resided in Port Dalhousie for nearly a century and half contributing economically, politically and socially.

"As kids, we'd go into Mrs. Couchouron's and get some newspapers. She had a little store down there by Marie's Seafood, towards Dalhousie House. We'd get a half dozen newspapers and pretend that we were paperboys in order to get into the grandstand to sell these papers."

Colin Johnston Sr. reflecting on childhood shenanigans

Lawrence Bentz

Lawrence Bentz, born in Port Dalhousie in 1912, is the great-grandson of the legendary 19th Century local fisherman "Dutch Pete" Nath. He moved away in 1920 to fish Lakes Superior, Nipigon and other interior lakes. This vibrant and colourful 87-year-old returned in 1936 and continues to live here today.

"In a matter of two years they were gone. Nobody ever knew what happened to them."

Lawrence Bentz on the disappearance of herring from Lake Ontario

George Graham

Born in Port Dalhousie in 1928, Mr. Graham lived here until age 26. His father was the Clerk and Treasurer of the village for 25 years and also ran a coal and ice business prior to 1935. As a boy, Mr. Graham worked for the lighthouse keeper Edmund 'Salty' Rooney.

"The Department of Transport had recently changed the fog horn sound, and instead of a deep bass, it had a higher pitch more akin to the horn at Port Weller. It seems Captain George Wilson assumed he was in the wrong spot and turned in search of Port Dalhousie!"

George Graham, regarding the day the Northumberland ran aground.

Jack Stunt

Jack Stunt, born in 1917, had music in his blood at an early age. As a teenager, he played tenor saxophone in a 7-piece orchestra on the cruise ship, "Northumberland" which ferried people between Port Dalhousie and Toronto. He played with Clarence Colton and continues to blow horn professionally today with a Niagara based big band.

"One Sunday morning I remember the girls from the Roxy, a burlesque house on Queen Street in Toronto, came over for a picnic. They rehearsed their midnight show for Sunday and we played for them. They didn't strip or anything. We were 17 & 18 year old kids, and that was exciting."

Jack Stunt, recalling days playing in a band on the cross-lake ferry

Ethel Williamson

Mrs. Williamson, born in 1907, is the author of three books and has had articles published in Good Housekeeping, Family Herald, Reminisce, Reader's Digest, and has been recently selected to be included in a Canadian anthology of writers on the Great Lakes. She was a stringer for the Standard and the Toronto Star and spent several years with her husband and their two boys tending the Port Weller Lighthouse.

"There was a bathhouse facing the beach, where one could rent a bathing suit for 25 cents. These suits were thin cotton jersey, usually gray with a red trim. Women wore bras under their suits and long stockings, rolled at the knee with round garters. Later, some men dared to wear trunks without tops, but they had to pay a fine."

Ethel Williamson, on swimming at Lakeside Park around 1915

Joyce Dunn and Vera Dudley

Mrs. Dudley was born in 1914 and her sister Mrs. Dunn was born in 1919.
They grew up in St. Catharines and as children and teenagers were frequent visitors to Port Dalhousie, hitching a ride or travelling by streetcar. Mrs. Dunn met her future husband at the dancehall in the park.

"Youngsters could go alone and we were given 5 cents for the fare down, 5 cents to come back and 5 cents to spend. We'd go around there all day deciding where to spend this nickel until it was time to get the streetcar."

Vera Dudley, recalling visiting Lakeside Park during the depression years

Harry Harper, James Harper, Ruth Harper, Marjorie Dawson

The Harper family was one of many families to settle in St. Catharines via the 'underground railroad' arriving in 1824 from South Carolina. The family was active with the huge Emancipation Day picnics held in Lakeside Park and, to this day, continue to celebrate the occasion with a smaller but significant family picnic.

"The part that always sticks with me is when we were about 13 or 14 and getting interested in girls. Every time we'd meet a good looking girl we'd try to shine up to her, and just when you got to the part of when you were holding hands someone would come up and say 'don't you know who that is? That's your cousin . . . ."

Harry Harper, explaining a common dilemma at the Emancipation Day picnics

Mary Patrick

Mrs. Patrick was born on December 1, 1937 and presently lives in St. Catharines with husband D'arcy. She grew up on Canal Street above her father's canoe livery of which she speaks of fondly. She taught at St. Ann School and raised seven children.

"There was a dancing platform that was always full of young people and fiddle music on weekends. His brothers were musical and they performed for the eager crowds. It was all very gay and festive."

Mary Patrick, talking about her father's canoe livery on Martindale Pond

Claude "Sandy" Saunders

Claude "Sandy" Saunders, born in 1913, has enjoyed an illustrious career in the field of rowing. He rowed professionally from the age of 18 to 36 and was spare man for the Canadian team that rowed in the Olympic Games in London, England in 1948. He has been elected to the prestigious Canadian Sports Hall of Fame in Toronto.

"Bill Thoburn was a professional gambler. He'd take all the bets in the grandstand—crews against crews. I can still see Bill with the money between his fingers."

Claude Saunders, recalling the prolific gambling at the Henley

The Dearly Departed

Jack Kellar, 1909-1989

As a boy he roamed the streets of Port Dalhousie going from one adventure to another. Having no place to go at night, he and his friends would visit Chief Smiley at his shanty and be a captive audience to his many tales.

Rhoda Abel, 1889-1982

Mrs. Abel was born and raised in Port Dalhousie. She and her family lived on a quarter acre of land where they grew potatoes, cabbage, turnips, carrots, and celery. She was a high spirited women who loved to play the piano.

Nellie Hare, 1896-1985

A sweet, soft-spoken lady, she lived at her home on the bank of the pond and regaled visitors with her girlhood tales as though they had happened just yesterday.

THE VILLAGE, EARLY IN THE CENTURY
COLIN JOHNSTON

*T*he Johnston Family has resided in Port Dalhousie for nearly a century and a half, contributing to the town as businessmen, politicians, and active participants in rowing, yachting, church and many other aspects of the community. Mr. Colin Johnston Sr. and his wife Gloria have resided at their home on Main Street for 43 years. They have five children, twelve grandchildren and one great-grandchild.

The following is a transcription of an interview with Mr. Johnston in which he recalls some family history and many details of his experiences living in Port Dalhousie.

COLIN JOHNSTON:

Early Family Enterprises

My great uncle had a shoe business on Front Street (Lakeport Road) where they manufactured leather handmade shoes and sold them to the sailors going through the Second Welland Canal. That's the one below the hill by the side of the Legion. They would take orders from the sailors on their way up and have the shoes ready for them on their way back down. It was quite a thriving business. My grandfather was not a shoemaker. He worked as a blacksmith in a shop at Lock and Main.

My father had a varied career. As a boy, he started working at the (Maple Leaf) Rubber Factory which is now Lincoln Fabrics. He got fifty cents a day and he was working along with the men. Dad was an ambitious person so he figured that he was doing the same work as the

First flag raising ceremony, Port Dalhousie Public School c.1877

men and should get the same pay which was $1.50. So he went to the boss, put his information in front of him and asked to be paid the same as the men. This fellow was a hard old nut and he said, "As long as you're a boy, you'll get a boy's pay. Go back to work!" He needed the job, so he did. Then he went to South Africa to the Boer War. When he came back they gave him a certificate for a quarter section of land in Western Canada. He went out to see what was available, but it did not appeal to him. He sold his certificate, came back to Ontario and went sailing for five summers on a package freighter called the St. Paul.

In 1911, he bought the coal business from a man named George Hicks. It was down on the far side of the harbour on the Michigan side. The coal was for domestic use only. If you ever want to dig over in that area, you'd probably find coal that's still in the ground. He was in the coal business for a year or two and found that there was a demand for ice. When they'd get good cold weather, they'd cut natural ice on the pond, put it in the icehouse and cover it over with straw. In the warm weather, they'd dig it out and deliver it door to door. That was before my time.

In the fall of 1931, the Department of Health wouldn't let them cut anymore ice off the canal because the water was polluted. My dad had to put in electrically operated machinery that made ice out of city water. He converted the old icehouse into an artificial ice plant. They called it artificial but it wasn't. It was real ice, but made artificially.

They'd put these cans into brine which was cooled by ammonia coils that ran through the water. These cans would hold approximately 300 lbs. of ice. After, they'd put them in a little tank to thaw the ice away from the container and then dump them out into a storage unit. It was cooled by ammonia coils up in the ceiling so it was cold in there. We could store 300 tons of ice in this big room. There was an elevator to lift the ice up as it became full, tier by tier. There were about 12 tiers in there. When things got better after the war, we built another room about the same size. In the early spring, when the demand wasn't that great, we'd fill up the big building making ten tons a day so that when the hot weather came, we'd have some reserve. We used wood shavings for insulation which we got for nothing from Davis Lumber. It was quite an operation. We delivered to Port Dalhousie, St. Catharines, Jordan, Vineland and wherever we could sell it. This went on until 1950. The electric refrigerator was being built for domestic use and when they became readily available, the ice business went downhill.

My dad was reeve of Port Dalhousie in the early 1920s and he was warden of the county in 1926. My brother was reeve of the town, warden of the county, and one of the early mayors . (The late R.M. Johnston, a former Member of the Ontario Legislature.) Those two were the politicians in the family. I didn't get into politics.

I first started in the insurance business in 1946 and in 1952 I decided to get a real estate broker's license. At that time Port Dalhousie was not too popular with the mortgage companies. It was very difficult to get a first mortgage. Some people had the wrong impression. They felt Port Dalhousie was going to be washed away by the lake or some ridiculous thing. The lakeshore was eroding and a lot of the bank would come down and take a bunch of trees with it. They did cure that problem and Port Dalhousie is still here.

The Old Henley Grandstand

The old grandstand used to be opposite Rennie Park. It was open and there was no roof on it. As kids, we'd go into Mrs. Couchouron's and get some newspapers. She had a little store down there by Marie's Seafood, towards Dalhousie House. We'd get a half dozen newspapers and pretend that we were paperboys in order to get into the grandstand to sell these papers. They were old newspapers. As soon as we got through the gate, we'd dispose of the papers and go watch the races.

The grandstand got so dilapidated that they pulled it down. It was getting pretty shaky. My dad was involved with the building of the new one around 1928.

Visitor Accommodation

Gloria Johnston: In the summertime my grandmother boarded people who'd come over from Toronto. They'd come year after year, stay with her for two or three weeks. And some of them hated to go home. One lady owned a hat factory in Toronto and others would come with small children. It was the same idea as the bed and breakfasts.

Rooms for rent to summer people was quite a popular enterprise. At the foot of Main Street there was a whole bunch of shacks and cottages (Gary Road). All down in there, below the hill, were all these little dwellings with one or two rooms. It was called Berryville because a family by the name of Berry owned it. People used to come over on the boat and rent those places for a weekend. Mostly they were vacant in the winter. One or two of them were well constructed and there was a man and his son that lived year - round in one of them.

Port Dalhousie (McArthur) Public School

Originally the school was called Port Dalhousie Public School and was located at the corner of Main and Ann Streets. There was a man by the name of George McArthur that came here as principal. The poor soul taught for two or three years and died in office while he was teaching. He was a well-liked man and when he died they felt sorry for him, so they changed the name from Port Dalhousie Public School to McArthur. He wasn't a local and he hadn't been here that long.

War Memorial Cenotaph

The soldiers' monument was erected in 1924 and my dad was reeve of the town at that time. The money for that was all raised by public subscription by the local people. There was no tax money in that. People dug into their pockets and donated. My dad started that and pushed for it. It was erected in memory of the soldiers that didn't make it through W.W.I. The soldier on the top is properly dressed with the Canadian army uniform. It was built six years after the war and they wanted to make sure that they had it all right. Wilfred Hart, a friend of my father's and a W.W.I veteran who had lost a leg in the war, was consulted. Dad and Wilfred went to Toronto where the stonecutters were carving this soldier. Wilfred made sure that all the uniform was accurate down to every detail.

The Jail

The jail had two cells. I remember as a kid getting up on a box and looking in a window and they had a prisoner in there. It could have been a local or maybe a sailor. This would have been in the early 1920s. The local constable was in the process of locking this fellow up and I remember him lighting the fire. They had a Quebec heater in there to provide a little heat. The prisoner was behind bars and he couldn't get out to the stove so the constable had to stoke the fire that would last all night. In the morning, they'd take him up to court and the judge would probably fine him $5 and tell him to get out of town. ¤

THE PROHIBITION YEARS
JACK KELLAR

*O*n September 15, 1916, presumably just prior to midnight, the last drink for the next eleven years was served. The Ontario Temperance Act (OTA), prohibiting the sale of alcohol, went into effect immediately after. From that moment on, the only way to purchase spirits legally was from a drugstore and only with a doctor's prescription. Needless to say, this system was abused and long line-ups occurred during the Christmas season. The OTA restricted sales within the province but it did not apply to purchases made outside the province. Prohibition was a provincial decision and Quebec chose not to outlaw the consumption of alcohol.

As a result, distillers and brewers took advantage of this loophole and opened warehouses and sales offices in Quebec. Liquor was manufactured in Ontario, shipped to Quebec and sold through the mail to residents of Ontario. One report was that no less than five boxcar loads of spirits were leaving daily from Montreal to Ontario. This did not go unnoticed and soon the federal government put a stop to it. The OTA remained in effect until 1927.

In 1920, the United States instituted a national prohibition that lasted until 1933 and many individuals became engaged in bootlegging and smuggling. Those who wished to transport liquor from Canada to the U. S. engaged the services of sailors, fishermen, farmers, and stunt pilots.

Clever schemes for conveying the contraband often met with the law. It would cross the border by road or more commonly by water. Boats of all types and sizes were employed. They would load up and then take out clearance papers for Cuba or Mexico, with no intention of ever making that destination. The Government Revenue Cruiser would stand guard to prevent the illicit transportation of liquor, and boats were seized regularly, their cargo confiscated and the crew fined heavily and, in some cases, imprisoned. The profits, as well as the risks, were high. Fortunes were made and many lives were lost as bootleggers battled with each other for control of liquor supplies and markets. Others died in confrontations with the authorities. During the 1920s, more that one million gallons of liquor each year were smuggled into the United States from Canada.

The late Mr. Jack Kellar (1909-1989) provided these insights on prohibition and rum-running as he remembered it as a boy living in Port Dalhousie.

JACK KELLAR:

Transporting The Goods

Liquor was out in Ontario, but it wasn't in Quebec. They used to send down to Quebec and they would send a boxcar load up. It would stop at the station on the Michigan side. Well, the Provincial Police would be there. I was never down there when they did it. The rumrunners used to hire the Michigan kids (those living on the east side of the harbour) to go down and open those cases and put all those bottles from the boxes into burlap bags. Then they were loaded into motor boats. At the customs office they'd get clearance papers for Cuba. Well as long as they didn't stop, they were all right. But the minute they stopped, either Canadian or US authorities could arrest them. They would run down to Olcott and some of the fishermen from Olcott would come out and meet them. Anyway they'd transfer the load and be back in a couple hours, load up again, and get clearance for Cuba. The same boat! Certainly they noticed it. Who cared?

There was this American house carpenter and he built a boat like a house. It had a flat bottom and the portholes were stationary. You couldn't open them. Well he brought it down to Port Dalhousie and he was going to go into the rum running business. He put a motor out of a truck in it or something and loaded up. Well, he was very inexperienced. He started out about high noon in his little boat—you could have paddled a canoe faster than this thing could move. It was chugging out of the pier and instead of turning towards the east, he turned towards the west. The Provincial Police were down there. They watched him go out and they saw him turning west. Well, they were sitting on the shore of the Fifteen when he came in. Now what his idea was, I don't know. He was apparently going to come in here, maybe meet someone and load it in a car and take it someplace else.

Trixies And Dollies

There were a lot of characters that moved into Port as a result. I lived next door to the Captain of one of those rumrunners, and he had a crew there. They were good neighbours. All the crewmembers had 'sisters' and 'cousins' that would come and visit them. These 'sisters' and 'cousins' were all named 'Dolly' or 'Trixie'. Some of the school girls started bobbing their hair and fixing up. The teacher would say, 'Now where'd you learn that?' 'Well so and so's cousin Trixie or so and so's sister Dolly, wears her hair this way'.

These women, even on the hottest day of summer, would have more rings and jewelry on than you could put in a trunk and they all wore red fox furs around their necks. Even on the hottest days! We accepted these people, at the time. I'm talking about us school kids. We were very naive. As far as we were concerned, yes these girls were the sisters and cousins of these fellows. We didn't know any different. Let's put it that way. Of course, now when you look back you can see they were cheap and trashy. But what comparison did the Port Dalhousie kids have? We had never seen anything like that before. The ladies chewed gum, spoke in slang and drove around in the fellows' fancy cars. When they passed the Public School, they'd wave and all the kids would wave back and say 'there goes so and so's cousin Trixie'. It never occurred to us that they were all named Trixie and Dolly. No one really cared. They were all good people and never did us any harm.

The gangsters were killing one another in the streets at that time. Not unlike what was happening in Chicago with Capone and his gangs. That type had their day. But one thing about the ones that came around here—they were all outsiders. The rumrunners were model citizens in Port Dalhousie. There was no trouble. They wanted no trouble. You know, they would step off the sidewalk and let you go by, before they would argue the point with you. And they were very polite. I cannot stress this enough. The girls with them were very polite, too. That's one thing I will say about them. The girls were, let's face it, we know what they were. But, on the other hand they were nice girls. There was no trouble with them. They never threw any wild parties and they were very quiet. They obeyed every law because it was a safe town. The Port Dalhousie people weren't going to bother them, and they weren't going to cause any trouble.

The Bootleggers

They were called rumrunners, but it wasn't actually rum. It was bottles of beer and wine. You got $15 a trip. That was about the wages they gave.

There were a lot of barges running through the canal at that time. They were all French Canadians on them. There was a Frenchman that lived down there, and of course he was a helper as he could speak French. He was buying bottles from these Frenchmen and storing them up for Christmas time. He sold it all year round, but at Christmas if you wanted a bottle of liquor it would cost $12 or $15. Well, there were fools who thought they couldn't celebrate Hogmanay without a bottle of liquor. They'd go around to Louis', get a bottle and pay any price from $12 to $15 depending how drunk he was. Well, he never left the house. If he did, his wife was there and they very rarely went out together. They were getting things ready because it was in the fall of the year—October or November.

I remember one glorious night in Port. There was this certain gang—not kids but adults and they spotted him and his wife going uptown. Up to St. Catharines. They watched them get onto the streetcar, rounded up some of those Michigan fellows and then broke into his house through a cellar window. They sounded like an army tank going through. That's how quiet they were. They shoved the smallest one in the window and then he came up and opened the door. They went in and carted all those cases out. They carted it over to the main street, by Alex Humphrey's store and the church minister was across the street. The liquor was piled there and everybody simply had to have a drink. Well everybody on the street heard them break in and saw them carrying it out. And people that never had a drink in their life had a drink. By the time Louis and his wife got home, what could they do? They couldn't report it to the police because it was illegal to have liquor in your house. And they had it by the case full! It was Saturday night and everybody that drank at all in Port was stoned drunk Sunday morning. People that had never had a drink weren't very far behind. And most people thought that was the biggest joke yet. Not too many people liked Louis anyway.

Charlie Moore, a bootlegger up in the old camps, and I were traveling together at the time and every Friday we went to see a Mr. Marshal (a local bootlegger). We had to be up there at half-past-four sharp. Not before and not after. It was like something out of a movie. We took an express cart up and we went around to the back and rapped at the back door. They had a wooden outside door with a pane of glass and a face would appear. 'What do you want kid?' And we'd say, 'Hey mister, those empty bottles?' Then he'd say, 'Just a minute'. And you'd hear the other door slam. 'Okay kids, it's under the veranda of the back porch'.

Well there'd be bags and bags of empty wine bottles and we'd load them all up. 'Get them out of here. Don't stop! Don't stop! Get them all out of here'.

A couple of times he'd come out and say, 'Here's a full bottle! Drop this off at such and such a place for me. And don't tell anybody!'

We were twelve years old (1921) at the time. Fifteen at the most. One time we got up there on a Friday and it was very, very muddy. We'd had lots of rain and of course the driveway was mud and this damned cart was loaded. Charlie and I were pulling and pushing this thing through the mud. A guy came out that looked just like your typical gangster. I forget which one but either Dolly or Trixie came out. She had on high heel shoes and jewelry hanging around her neck, and all these rings and a fox fur around her neck. What a sight! This old guy was helping Charlie pull at the front and we were pushing at the back. We got it out on the road and away we went. Her in her high heels, silk stockings and fancy short dress. Well, when I say short, all I can say is that styles were different. Just below her knee. And she had enough rouge on her to stop a bullet. Of course, Charlie and I thought she was pretty nice to come out and help us like that. There weren't too many Port girls that would have done that. Of course, these girls were quite frequently changing. But they were always 'Trixie' or 'Dolly'. They were very quiet and never bothered anyone.

This Mr. Marshal—now that may be his name and may not—was apparently asked by police what he did for a living. He said he peddled meat around the village. Well, then he had to show that he was peddling meat. So then he had to establish a route. He was a smart old fellow. He got an old truck and he started peddling meat around the village. The first time he came around our district, my grandmother went outside and she said. 'How much is such and such?' And he told her. She said, 'My goodness, I could buy at Scott and Murphy's cheaper than that'. She had a small hand purse in her pocket, and she took it out and had it in her hand. He took it out of her hand and opened it up. There was about seventy-five cents in it and he said, 'Is that all you got?' And he put it in his pocket and he said, 'Okay, now I'll give you seventy-five cents worth'. He then put a very large roast

in her hand, and sausages, wieners, and
who knows what all. Then he said,
'Now look old woman, I'm a busy man
and I can't argue with you all day for
the sake of seventy-five cents. I'm too
busy'. He peddled meat in Port
Dalhousie for quite awhile. He'd say,

'How much money have you got? I want fifty-cents for that'. 'They
shot Jesse James for being a robber, you know,' the man replied. 'All
right, you want a sausage? Take it and get out of my darn life'. And
he'd just pick it up, and hand it to him. He wouldn't wrap it or
anything. 'I'm a busy man. I haven't time to bother with you'.

He was very quiet and never bothered anybody. Every once in
awhile he'd carry out a bag of empty bottles. We'd come over Friday
and there'd be a bag of empty bottles. And then one night he wasn't
there. They came in the night and left in the night.

One time Captain Tony and I got talking and I asked him what
happened to old Charlie. 'Oh he resigned. He left here and went down
to the States. He was shot in one of those gang wars or something'.
And I asked him what happened to Mr. Marshal and he said, 'Why
don't you mind your own business?'.

I remember I was working at Fort Erie and two of us went into a
place. They were bootleggers and I don't drink. And my friend said,
'Give him a bottle of beer'. And this woman sitting there said, 'What's
the sense giving him a beer? He don't drink anyway'. And he said,
'How do you know?' 'Oh I know Jack from way back'. And it was
this Dolly or whoever she was, that helped us push the cart.

And you know a funny thing, every time Charlie and I went to Mr.
Marshal's for a load of bottles he'd come out and give us a temperance
lecture before he'd give them to us. He did. He'd say, 'Look at all
these bottles. Fools! Fools buy that stuff. I don't drink. I make money
and sell that stuff to fools that do. Look at how they throw their money
away. You kids don't drink now. Don't ever drink.' He'd go on about
liquor and he'd say, 'if you're going to handle liquor, sell it. Don't
drink it'. ¤

THE FISHING INDUSTRY
LAWRENCE BENTZ

*D*uring the latter part of the 19th century and the early part of the 20th century, Port Dalhousie hosted a vibrant fishing industry. Little evidence remains of the community that once occupied what is now Lakeside Park, save for some rare photographs and a few mementos saved from those bygone days.

Mr. Lawrence Bentz was born in 1912 into a family of fishermen. His great-grandfather is the legendary 19th century local fisherman 'Dutch Pete'. In 1920, Mr. Bentz moved away with his family to fish Lake Superior, Lake Nipigon and other interior lakes. He returned in 1936 to resume fishing and lives here in the old town to this day.

LAWRENCE BENTZ:

The Fishing Community

I come from a family of fishermen. Dutch Pete, my grandfather, my father and myself were all fishermen. Dutch Pete came here from Pennsylvania and built a house on the east side of the harbour where the inner lighthouse now stands. He raised two daughters; one daughter

Dutch Pete

married John Peter Bentz who was my grandfather. They raised two children and they lived out along the beach on the west side of the harbour along with other families—the DeLucas, the Brooks, the Johnstons . . . .

The Johnston family was quite well known. Ike Johnston, the grandfather who first lived on the beach, he was the grandfather of

Robert Johnston who later became the Reeve of Port Dalhousie, the mayor of St. Catharines and an M.L.A. The time I am speaking about would be around Dutch Pete's time and my grandparents' time, sometime between 1850 and 1914.

When they filled in the original canal, they left an area called a slip about 150 yards long, north of where the Port Mansion is now. It emptied into the harbour and was probably 20 to 30 feet wide. This is where the commercial fishermen had their boats. They had their fishing shanties all along the banks as well as their reels for drying the nets.

Their boats were all open boats. There were no wood cabins on them and they were probably anywhere from 20 to 36 feet long. Some had been sailboats before they put in the gas engines because they still had their centreboards. They were all mostly what they called 'clinker built' boats; that is, the planks all overlapped one another from the keel to the gunnels. The edges of the planks prevented them from rolling too much. They were like narrow fins that would catch the water. They were built mostly of cedar or cypress on oak frames. Even though they had engines, they all had a provision to sail. They had what they call a 'leg-o-mutton' sail. It was just a single sail they could hoist if anything went wrong with the engine. They had oars and, if the boat was too big to use oars, they had one sculling oar. This is something that you don't see anymore, but something relative to what gondoliers use in Venice.

The fishermen were divided, that is to say that some were inshore fishermen. This is no reflection on their courage or anything like that. It was probably due to what equipment they had. The inshore fishermen fished primarily for pickerel and shore herring but, on occasion, would go out and fish for whitefish. The whitefish were usually in deeper water.

The offshore fishermen also fished inshore. Primarily they fished for whitefish, deep shore herring, ciscoes, and lake trout. Most of the whitefish were caught in what they call a 'one-night fish'. That meant that the nets were only allowed to stay down one night. Sometimes because of a storm or something, we couldn't get out to lift them. They'd be down two nights but we'd get them in as soon as possible. I'm saying 'we' because this was in later years when I was fishing with my father. In the fall of the year, the herring run was so great that there were fishermen from Niagara-on-the-Lake. There was Daddy Ball, Taffy Ball, Johnny Ball, Sid Gogo, the Master brothers and Johnny Bolton. There were two steam tugs that would come down from Grimsby with the Hand brothers. Charlie and Fred DePew used to come across from the north shore over in Bowmanville. That's how lucrative it was. The boats would come in so loaded with fish almost to the point of being dangerous with not enough freeboard.

The fish were taken out of the nets and the nets were taken back and set again for the next night. A lot of the herring went to Toronto, but if they had some left, well then they were all scaled and cleaned in the afternoon and at night. Even as a little boy, they used to set me up on a stool and I would scale herring while my mother and my grandmother cleaned them. Then they were washed and put in a salt brine that was strong enough to float an egg.

They were left in the brine overnight, taken out in the morning, washed and salted down in kegs and firkins. A firkin was a wooden tub that lard used to be sold in. They were salted down—a layer of fish—a layer of salt—a layer of fish—a layer of salt, and then stacked away in the shanty. In the winter they were taken out and freshened and smoked. This was the winter cash flow. If the fishermen did not get jobs in the dry dock—lots of them had to spend the winter mending their nets—they would smoke fish and go up and sell them at the St. Catharines' market.

The buyers were so anxious to buy Lake Ontario whitefish for the markets in New York, they'd come up here in the spring of the year. I can still see them carrying their valises. They'd come down and visit the fishermen in their shanties and they'd have these valises loaded with liquor, silk stockings, chocolates and cigars. Well, my father never drank or smoked, but my grandfather and Dutch Pete did.

It was a matter of a handshake. 'Yes, we'll send your fish to you, Star Fish Co., 36 Peck Slip, Fulton Market, New York'. I can still remember it!

This time period would be probably from early 1900 up until 1920-21 when the herring simply disappeared. In a matter of two years they were gone. Nobody ever knew what happened to them and, of course, they did not have the environmentalists and biologists that are here today to investigate these things. But in a matter of two years, like I said, they were gone. The lake herring did come back a little bit around 1936-37-38 but nothing like what they were.

I met a lot of fishermen as a boy. Jimmie Doig, George, Charlie and Jimmie Elliot, George Julian, Harry Reece, Ed Rooney, Peter, Phil, and Eddie Nath, Ed McNulty, Chauncey Thomas and his sons Dave and Bill, and my own family John Bentz Sr., John Jr. and Jack.

Later, as I grew older, I wasn't always a fisherman. I've had a varied career. When I went up north, I went up there as a fisherman. But I also worked in the lumber camps, worked for the Federal Government catching fish for Indians—Ontario Forestry Branch, as a trapper.

When my dad was fishing on the north shore of Lake Ontario, in the mid 1920s, we used to visit an old salt and lake fisherman named Captain Johnny Goldring. He was crusty and rough around the edges and had a theory on the disappearance of the herring from Lake Ontario. He believed that there were deep caverns in Lake Ontario and that the herring went down into them and somehow could not find their way out. My father was never convinced of this.

A Fisherman's Day

The fishermen would be up and at their shanties by 6:00 or 6:30 a.m. They would lift the nets by hand. This is before they had mechanical lifters. If it wasn't blowing too hard or wasn't too big a sea running, they'd leave the harbour by a quarter of seven. A lot did leave even earlier so they'd have the fish ready to ship to Toronto on the first passenger boat which landed here around 10 a.m. They'd go out and lift the nets, and by that I mean they'd pull them into the boats. Sometimes they'd clear the fish out of the nets. You've heard the expression 'herring chokers'? They'd squeeze them so the fish slipped through the web of the net without tearing the mesh. The more nets you tore, the more mending you had to do in the wintertime. They would bring them in and clean them if they had to be shipped cleaned. The gills would be taken out, the bellies opened up and the entrails taken out. Then they'd be packed in ice and shipped.

All the fish shipped to the Fulton Market in New York City for the Jewish trade had to be shipped 'round'. That meant not cleaned. It had something to do with their religion. Same as they preferred fish with big scales. They would not eat eel. No way!

All we had to do was put them on the train with the address and they were shipped through Niagara Falls, and Buffalo. The New York Central picked them up and the express was paid down there. They were all shipped on consignment and sold by auction. Afterwards they would send us a cheque. I don't think anybody was ever beat. The buyers wouldn't take that chance because if they did, they'd never get anymore fish.

Before shipping, our names were all stamped on the boxes and on the cards that were put on the boxes. Some of the fishermen were shipping fish that weren't as fresh as they should have been. Sometimes the fish were out in the nets for two nights instead of one, and the water would be warm. They weren't bad, but, they weren't as fresh as the others.

I've seen a whole deck load of fish go sour in a matter of two hours, particularly whitefish. I can't explain it to you. They hadn't been cleaned and it wasn't a case of half cleaning them and leaving some of the guts in.

The fish that was bound for Toronto, went by boat. There were two boats, the Dalhousie City and the Northumberland that plied back and forth during the summer. They carried passengers, as well as packaged freight and fruit.

After the fish were cleared from the nets, some of the fishermen would put the nets up on reels to dry. It was work that they didn't really have to do. The fishermen felt if they put them back wet they tore too much web. They could set nets a lot faster if they weren't wet, but there was a lot more work attached to that. Others would take them back out and set them wet. The nets were made of cotton and linen. Every ten days, or whenever they needed it, the nets had to be cleaned. The slime was washed off the nets with slaked lime.

The fishermen didn't make all their nets. They mended them. But when you wanted new nets you bought what was called the web. The web was the basic part of the nets. Like if you look at a fence, the top line is the cork line and the bottom line is the lead line. The middle part is known as the web. You'd buy the line separate, you'd buy the seaming twine separate and you'd buy the web separate. Now it had to be what they called seamed or hung on the main lines of the net. And they'd string the lines up and stretch them real tight so that they wouldn't stretch after, because if they did, then that would put out the hang of the net.

My mother was very fast when it came to sewing the web on the line. They brought a man from Port Maitland named Charlie Troutwine. He thought he was going to challenge my father to see how fast they could both seam. He was supposed to be the fastest seamer on Lake Erie. My mother beat the pants off him! The people from Fort Erie lined up on one side and the people from Port Dalhousie lined up on the other. They did three stretches and mum beat him. But he was a good sport.

The Thing About 'Ling'

There was a fish we could never use. It was called ling. They had a tail like an eel and a flat head. They were supposed to be what they called 'freshwater cod'. They were a nuisance. We couldn't market them. They had a skin on them and they'd scare the life out of you. They looked a lot like a catfish only they were big. They were mottled brown, green, gray, all sorts of colours. The tail would go through one mesh, come out and go through another, go through another and before they were finished they had what we call a snarl in their mouth. It would be the web all tangled up as thick as my finger or thicker. And that had to be all picked out again because it would take up an area of the web which couldn't be used to fish. You were deprived of that much area of your net to fish. And it had to be all picked out and untangled before you could set the nets back.

The ling liver oil was very high in vitamins—more vitamins than in cod liver oil. The northern lakes were full of them and the Government was going to set up a factory that would extract the oil from the liver but the East coast lobbied and stopped it. But if they had ever set up a factory to extract the oil out of ling, a lot of fishermen, including myself, would have been rich, rich people. You could catch them by the ton. By the ton! But we had no use for them.

An evocative portrait of 'Dutch' Pete Nath taken on the Port Dalhousie beach where he lived and made his living c.1894

Steamer 'Empress of India' on the west pier at the N.S.&T. terminal c.1884

THE CROSS-LAKE FERRIES
COLIN JOHNSTON, GEORGE GRAHAM, JACK STUNT

*I*n 1884, the first cross-lake ferry service was established between Toronto and Port Dalhousie. The service continued with a variety of vessels up until 1950 and many still fondly remember the latter days of the era. The expansive beach at Port Dalhousie was the main draw for people coming from Toronto. Likewise, the City of Toronto offered an exciting day trip for Niagara residents.

Colin and Gloria Johnston reflect on their experiences aboard the steamers Northumberland and Dalhousie City. George Graham, born in 1928 and raised on Main Street in Port Dalhousie, recalls one particular foggy but eventful day. St. Catharines native, Jack Stunt, born in 1917 and a professional musician to this day, talks about his teenage years entertaining the passengers.

COLIN JOHNSTON:

The Sister Ships

We used to travel back and forth on the Northumberland. My mother came from Toronto and her mother and sisters used to come over on the Northumberland and Dalhousie City. In those days you could buy a book of tickets (12 trips) for five dollars. It was fifty cents a trip to cross the lake. Pretty cheap! The two ships would take a trip each. For example, the Northumberland wouldn't make more than one trip to Toronto and back in a day. But in-between the Northumberland's schedule, the Dalhousie City would go.

Gloria Johnston recalls: They used to have moonlight excursions. I remember those. Before I was married, I went over on the Dalhousie City with a friend. Of course we didn't drink in those days, but they had a band to dance to. After I got married (1941) my girlfriend and I would make a day of it and shop. We'd go over in the morning and get the late one back.

The farmers would ship their fruit on the Dalhousie City first thing in the morning. The freight train would come down here at ten o'clock at night loaded with fruit. It would be put in the freight shed that ran northerly from the ferry landing. The freight train would come in on one side of the shed and put the fruit in. Then they'd put it through to the other side and on the boat to Toronto in the morning. They used to go at 8:30 in the morning. You could set your clock by it. I can remember hearing the whistle blow. It was the signal that it was time to get to school. The Northumberland blew the whistle coming into the harbour at 4:30 p.m. That was the signal to get home for dinner. This would have been in the early 1920s and 1930s.

It was a catastrophic event for Port Dalhousie when the Northumberland burned on June 2, 1949. It fouled up the crossing of Lake Ontario by these two C.N.R. boats and put a hole in the tourist attraction for Lakeside Park. Year after year the ship was painted. That paint was great material to feed a fire. She was already to go for

Passengers board the side-wheeler 'Garden City' preparing to leave Harbour c.1915

the summer season. Somebody was a careless smoker and they set the thing on fire. They still had the Dalhousie City but she could only carry half the people. She ran for that next year. In 1950 she was sold to some outfit down in Lachine, Quebec and ran down on the river. Apparently, she burned as well the following year.

There was a fueling dock in the harbour. It fueled the ships before oil became prevalent in the engine rooms for powering the steam. They'd put soft coal into the bunkers of these ships. The coal would come down by freight cars. It was put up into this overhead thing and the lever would be pulled. When the coal hit the ship, the dust would go up almost like an atomic bomb.

GEORGE GRAHAM:

Lost In The Fog

The passenger steamer 'Northumberland' was a beautiful sight to see whenever she entered Port Dalhousie Harbour in the 1930s and '40s. It was delightful to sail even in rough waters. The boat's terrific maneuverability was due to its two propellers. They could be reversed for full back-up or if you just reversed one engine, the boat would turn in a circle.

The Northumberland made one very memorable entry into the Port that I will never forget. It was a foggy day in 1942 after a night when our lightkeeper, Mr. Edward Rooney, had to stay up looking after the foghorn. A sister ship, the Dalhousie City, made port safely in time for lunch, although the going was very slow. Suddenly, we heard five blasts from the Northumberland, somewhere in the distance. These repeated every few minutes. To our shock, she came in close to the piers, then veered west and hit ground opposite Albert Street (now Bayview).

The Department of Transport had recently changed the fog horn sound, and instead of a deep bass, it had a higher pitch more akin to the horn at Port Weller. It seems Captain George Wilson assumed he was in the wrong spot and turned in search of Port Dalhousie!

Everyone on shore was in a state of near panic. Mr. Rooney and others set out with the speed boat. Colin Johnston set out in the Reese fish boat. All shouted to the Northumberland that the Port Dalhousie piers were only five minutes sail time eastward from their present location.

The Northumberland ably reversed her engines, backed off the sand bar, and turned eastward. Incredibly, she went right past the piers and ran aground once more, nearly half way to Port Weller! The passengers began shouting for help. This time the Dalhousie City, with its passengers now discharged, set out to meet the Northumberland. All passengers left the Northumberland and boarded its sister steamer.

It was several years after this eventful day when the Northumberland was destroyed by fire on June 2, 1949. Her whistle is still active today at the Marine Museum in Toronto. Hearing this 'blast from the past' at the museum is a sentimental reminder for me as I remember a great ship that met a sad end. ¤

Burning of the 'Northumberland' with sister ship Dalhousie City in foreground

JACK STUNT:

The Band On The Boat

As a teenager I was caught between music and sports. I played lacrosse and finally the music grabbed me. I worked at G.M. for almost 40 years as a Comptroller before taking an early retirement. All through the years I played at weddings every Saturday night. Music keeps me young.

When I was around 17 or 18 the Big Bands were coming on stream. I used to listen to them every night in bed. I played violin but just had to have a saxophone. There was a sax for sale in St. Catharines by a musician named Meighan who played in the Lincoln-Welland Band. It was an old sax and I bought it for $30.00. I took a lesson that same day after school from Leo Leisch who played with Clarence Colton. I remember my first dance was above The Standard and I got fifty cents for the night's play. Then I started to play in an eight piece local band.

In the early days everyone wanted three saxophones, a trumpet, drums, bass, piano and trombone. We used to play at church and lodge dances. Then I moved up the ladder. Eventually I started to play with Clarence Colton in the late 1930s. I was playing alto sax at that time. Also on sax was Leo Leisch and Merle Hill. We had some great musicians. There was Reg Ecclestone, Clarence's brother Frank from Port Dalhousie who played banjo, Gord Heaton on drums, and a bass player from Thorold named Joe Fairchild.

Prior to this time, when I was still in high school, the Northumberland and Dalhousie City were running back and forth between Toronto and Port Dalhousie. They always used Toronto bands, but for some reason they decided they had better use St. Catharines' bands as well. A band leader and violin player from St. Catharines named Bill Beaucock got the job. He basically just led the band. At any rate, I was chosen to play in the band along with Ralph Milligan on sax, Lorne Grewar, sax, Jack Phelan, trumpet, Doug Stoddard, piano and Bill Morris, bass violin.

When we'd be out on the lake and a good looking girl would come onto the bandstand, Bill Beaucock would open up his violin case and call for 'Melancholy Baby'. Well, we were all young guys and didn't want to play that old stuff. But we had to. One of Lorne Grewar's jobs was to make sure all of the instruments were on board, so he said, "I'll take care of this." The next time one of those good looking girls came on the dance floor we'd start to play 'Melancholy Baby' and Bill's string would break. This happened three weeks in a row. Lorne had been cutting one of the strings part ways through with a razor blade.

When I played on the Northumberland, it was around 1935. Beverage rooms had just been allowed and all the hotels were putting them in. So on Saturday we would get on the boat around 9 a.m. We didn't play on the way over because our engagement started in Toronto and wound up back in Toronto around 2:30 Sunday morning. We had two complete return trips. The crossing took approximately 2½ to 3 hours and we'd have around an hour and fifteen minutes before the first sailing. We'd run up to the Walker House on Front Street and have a couple of ten cent beers, come back, get on the boat and play. We were only kids then. When we got back to Port Dalhousie, we'd run up to the Port Hotel, have a couple more and run back.

One Sunday morning I remember the girls from the Roxy, a burlesque house on Queen Street in Toronto, came over for a picnic. They rehearsed their midnight show for Sunday and we played for them. They didn't strip or anything. We were 17 and 18-year-old kids, and that was exciting.

Besides playing every Saturday, we would do excursions to the old Toronto Maple Leaf Ball Park at the foot of York St. Somebody would organize an excursion and we would play for the dancing. They'd go out on the lake, maybe up the Niagara River and back around. Kind of fun things. I played two years there.

Port Dalhousie was a big drawing card. People from Toronto would come across for organized picnics in Lakeside Park. There was a dance hall with dances Saturday night. They would bring in Toronto bands, too, that played every night of the week. It was a dime a dance and we'd play two courses of a tune and quit. Then they'd let them out of the roped area and a new group with tickets would come in to dance. You got about five minutes for a dime. ¤

Dalhousie City

Northumberland

LAKESIDE PARK

COLIN JOHNSTON, ETHEL WILLIAMSON, VERA DUDLEY & JOYCE DUNN

*P*ort Dalhousie was once more famous for its park than it was for its canal. In fact, when the Welland Canal was relocated to Port Weller in 1932, Port Dalhousie continued to thrive as an even more popular tourist destination. The beach was wider in those years and Lakeside Park, with its midway, offered everything from games-of-chance to carnival rides to dancing. It was a great place to spend a summer's day.

No doubt, there are countless stories to be told of the fun times spent in the park—as children or as adults, during the day or after dark, with family or with friends—certainly enough to fill a book.

Colin and Gloria Johnston provide insights from their own experiences growing up a few blocks away from Lakeside Park. Ethel Williamson (born 1906) a published author who continues to write to this day, offers up delightful commentary recalling childhood days in the park. Vera Dudley (born 1914) and Joyce Dunn (born 1919), sisters and lifelong St. Catharines residents, recall first coming to the park as children and then as teenagers visiting the dancehall.

The midway in Lakeside Park running the length of the beach

COLIN JOHNSTON

American Visitors

The park was at its peak before the war. (W.W.II) People used to come over here from the United States by car. Big cars! Auburns, Cadillacs, Packards. We only had little Chevs and Fords around here. In the parking lot it cost fifteen cents to park all day. I can remember seeing a sixteen cylinder Caddy. It was a great big beautiful car. There was a gas pump down there and she took thirty gallons of gas, which was a lot of gas. Other cars would take, maybe, ten or fifteen.

Emancipation Day was a big day in the park and we always went down. We didn't want to miss anything. Some came by boat but mostly by car. They had barbecues set up on Lock Street as well as in the park. They had card games going like Three Card Monty. They had shell games which consisted of upside down shells on a board. A pea would be put under one shell and the man would say, "You see it now. That's where it is. Follow it and tell me where it is." And he'd go back and forth, back and forth. Nine out of ten times, they'd guess the wrong one. The big game for the black people on Emancipation Day was the crap shoot. They had a blanket and they'd lay it out on the grass in the park. There was a row of lights along the west end of the park. The police, trying to maintain law and order, would come along and tell these guys, "You can't do that." So, they'd pick up all their gear and the blanket, move along to the next light, spread it out again, and away they'd go. There was never any trouble. They were just there for fun.

On a Sunday, the parking lot used to get full at fifteen cents a car. Martin Howe used to park cars at his Uncle Harrigan's vacant lot at the corner of Lock and Main. My brother and I parked cars in a vacant lot my dad owned at the corner of Gertrude and Queen (Dalhousie Ave.). From there you'd go down one block, down the stairs and into the park. We were a little more expensive. We charged a quarter. ¤

The Attractions

Along the midway there was the Caterpillar, Hey Dey, Merry-go-round and other rides. There were all kinds of games like the fishpond and pull the string. Hot dogs, french-fries and popcorn were sold. And the Honey Dew stand was a favourite.

That was our summer entertainment. We couldn't afford to go to summer camp. We'd spend our summers in the park.

On the sand by the pier, there was a restaurant called the Lakeside Inn. It had a really nice dining room facing the water and they used to pack them in there. I think it burned down.

In the 1920s, there was a bathhouse down there and they rented bathing suits to people. There was a slide out there in the water. In the spring they'd pull it out there with a nine-team of horses. In the fall, a team would pull it back in. It was kept up on the beach. It was a great attraction for kids my age. We'd climb to the top of that thing and look around at the scenery.

In 1932, we had a big blow here. I was in, what they called in those days, entrance class (grade 8). The wind came up out of the north. There wasn't much wind surface to that slide and it blew that thing right up on the beach. So you can imagine how strong the wind was. It knocked a bunch of trees down on Main Street as well. Salty Rooney had a little concession at the beach with row boats to rent to tourists. Some of the row boats wound up in the trees.

Gloria Johnston: There was a dancehall in Lakeside Park. I wasn't allowed to go down on my own. My mother chaperoned me and a couple of girlfriends of mine. They had good name bands that played there. In those days we used to do the Lambeth Walk. There were words to it too. 'Doing the Lambeth Walk'. Then you'd clap.

When the Welland Ship Canal opened up in 1931, there was a drop in activity in Port Dalhousie because the ships, instead of coming through here, were down in Port Weller. But the park still remained a popular spot. She only started to die after the Northumberland burned on June 2, 1949.

Sid Brookson bought the park from the railway after the war. He used to bring the Lady Hamilton down here to run trips between Hamilton and Port Dalhousie. It was a ship owned by the Hamilton Harbour Commission and would bring picnickers from Dofasco and other companies. On Sundays, in between picnics, to kill time for a couple of hours they used to take trips out on the lake. They'd circle around and then come back in. It was just a boat ride, but they did have moonlight excursions. This was after the days of the Dalhousie City and Northumberland. ¤

ETHEL WILLIAMSON

A Day At The Beach

I was only five in 1912 when my parents took me to Port Dalhousie and I had my first ride on the merry-go-round, which we now call the carousel. I must admit, I was afraid! Riding the streetcar to Port Dalhousie became a regular event for our family, for picnics, on tables under shady trees; for watching fireworks on the 24th of May; sitting on the small grandstand, watching a baseball, football or soccer game on a playing field, east of the Park.

I was the eldest of four children and in turn, Dad taught all of us to swim in the lake. There was a bathhouse facing the beach, where one could rent a bathing suit for 25 cents. These suits were thin cotton jersey, usually gray with a red trim. Women wore bras under their suits and long stockings, rolled at the knee with round garters. Later, some men dared to wear trunks without tops, but they had to pay a fine.

A row of outhouses also faced the beach—large holes for adults, small ones for children. Years later a row of flush toilets was built along the left side of the park, and one paid a small amount for their use. By this time, there was a midway, running from the pavilion to the carousel. It was run by Mr. and Mrs. Brown. There was an airplane ride, bumper cars that one could steer and crash into others, and concession stands where one could buy fries, ice cream, soft drinks, candy floss and taffy apples.

In the early days the carousel was closer to the beach. In the winter, it was encased with wooden panels and locked up. The pavilion then was popular for Saturday dances, and behind it was a row of super swings. There was also a nice restaurant on the beach, close to the pier and overlooking the lake. There wasn't a covered picnic area, but lots of trees, shading picnic tables. Open streetcars brought thousands of people to the park, where they spent many happy hours.

That Water Slide

I remember when the water slide was placed in the lake. It was great! My sister Ann, who was ten at the time, loved going down to the park and sliding down the slide. One day she arrived there ahead of the rest of us and went down the slide. Again and again! Later, on the beach, she saw a young man walking very closely behind her. This went on for some way and she was afraid. She finally decided to confront him and she turned around to face him. He apologized, then said, "I was close to you because the seat of your swim suit has been worn off from your countless trips down the slide. I knew you would not want anyone to see your bare bottom." Ann never forgot this.

One day my little sister, Pearl, happened to be the first child to climb the steps for a slide. It was a hot, sunny day and she was unaware the slide was dry. Down she went, crying out all the way, for the dry wood had burned her bottom and legs. She even had slivers from the slide. The first person on the slide was to bring a hat full of water, to pour on, before going down. Once the slide was wet, it was safe to go down.

Special Moments

On summer holidays, my brother, James and I would take a lunch and spend the whole day at the beach. He was ten and I was twelve. We were both good swimmers, and liked diving off the wooden raft that was anchored out in the lake. Dad taught us how to float on our backs. One day while I was floating, two youths were watching.

When we got home, James told my parents that, after I had left, he followed the boys and heard them say I was a pippen! Mom and Dad were upset, but secretly, pleased. I thought it was a compliment; My very first!

Other outstanding events at Port Dalhousie were Bathing Beauty Contests, the renowned Emancipation Day, where black people gathered in the park to celebrate their freedom from slavery. The Hyfield Tennis Club attracted young folk from the Niagara District, for it had great courts and some champion players. I learned to play tennis there.

When Cy and I were courting we spent many happy hours at Port Dalhousie. Cy rowed with the Sea Cadets and had won several medals at the Henley Regatta, so we always went there. On the last night of the Regatta, it was time for celebrating. We always went to the Regatta Dance, held in the pavilion, with a great band, Clarence Colton and the Best, with Mr. Scout Coombs, Principal of the St. Catharines Collegiate, and his wife as host and hostess.

My most memorable event at Port was the night Cy proposed to me and gave me an engagement ring, while sitting on a concrete seat at the base of a pier light. As we kissed, the foghorn from the Lighthouse sent out a blast and we nearly jumped out of our skins. Was this a sign of our future life together? ¤

(Mrs. Williamson's husband, Cy, later became the Lighthouse Keeper at Port Weller. She referred to herself as the light housekeeper.)

JOYCE DUNN & VERA DUDLEY

The Dancehall In The Park

The dancehall located at the west end of the beach

Vera: We used to go to the dancehall when we were just kids. Everybody went to Port Dalhousie. That was the place to be. Really, there was no place else.

Joyce: We'd go for picnics, to swim and of course, to the dancehall. Live bands performed in the dance pavilion but only in the summer. Different bands played, but to us they were all great. A sax, drums, piano—about six piece. But of course there was no Sunday dancing. The girls would pay a dime to get in, have their hands stamped and the fellows had to pay a nickel a dance. They'd buy the tickets and then ask you to dance. Every time they took you on the floor, they'd give the ticket to a man that was standing there.

Just like going to the show and, naturally, they didn't play real long songs. The dance would end pretty quick for a nickel. That's where I met my husband. I was 16. He asked me to dance and then for a date. We didn't have money to spend, so we'd walk downtown and look in the store windows. Three years later we were married and I was never sorry a day. A lot of people met their future spouses there.

There was beautiful music played in the dancehall. Mostly waltzes and foxtrots. This was around 1934. Those were depression years and most of the fellows were lucky if they had the money to go. There were no chairs or places to sit. We just stood around and waited for someone to ask us to dance. The dance pavilion had flaps that opened up just like on a summer cottage. On the outside it was low enough for people to see in. And crowds of people stood watching. There was no drinking then. I think that was the best time because you never had to worry about people getting obnoxious or drinking and driving.

Getting There

Vera: We started going down to the park when I was ten or eleven. It was a beautiful park to go swimming at. The water was so clean. We never heard the word pollution in those days. It was a shame how that all happened and got out of control.

Joyce: We'd hitchhike down to Port. You could do that in those days. It was an ordinary thing. Everyone did it. We didn't always have money for carfare. But you didn't have to worry about hitchhiking in those days because it was usually somebody who knew you that picked you up. People that were taking their families down and they'd squeeze us in. I remember a chap that lived up the street who had a truck with an open back. He had a son and, once in awhile, he'd take a whole bunch of us down in his truck. We'd come up Ontario Street and it was all farms. All of us kids would get a couple of apples, or a couple of pears to eat on the way home. Nobody bothered you. We'd just be at the side of the road because we didn't want to miss a ride. If we had the money, we'd go on the streetcar for a nickel. We'd wait for the one with the open sides on it—the seats went straight across. The streetcar ran behind General Motors, over Martindale. It was a great ride for us.

My girlfriend Edie and I would go down quite often. One night we met these two chaps at the dancehall and they were going to give us a ride home. Well, we went out to this car and my girlfriend and I got in the back. It was an old Nash but there were no doors in the back. We got up Ontario Street, up around Lock 2 and she and I hung on to each other for dear life. That old wind was just a whistling across there. We thought we were going to go right out onto the road. There wasn't anything to hang on to.

Vera: Youngsters could go alone and we were given five cents for the fare down, five cents to come back and five cents to spend. We'd go around there all day deciding where to spend this nickel until it was time to get the streetcar.

Joyce: We'd take a sandwich with us and save that for a treat. In those days not many had cars, and family upon family would pack a picnic hamper and spend the whole day in Port Dalhousie. It was a very popular place. It's really hard to visualize what it was like. And there aren't a lot of pictures. Of course when we were kids we couldn't afford a camera. All the times we went to Port, I don't ever remember taking a picture.

People came to the park by streetcar

There was a great big slide out in the water. We loved to go on that. A young fellow was killed when he decided to dive off the top of it. Wasn't old enough to know better, I suppose. To us it seemed very high.

Vera: After they tore all those buildings down, I couldn't believe there had been so much on that midway in that space. Booth after booth on both sides. Games, rides, food, taffy apples, candy floss. The last thing was the carousel. I remember one game run by the McNulty's where you'd pull a string for a nickel and got whatever was on the end of it. We'd be hanging around for so long that once in awhile he'd feel sorry for us and let one of us pull it. We thought he was the greatest. That's the way people were in those days.

Joyce: It was the same with the streetcar. We'd wait for this one driver since we would spend all of our allowance and then have no way to get home except to hitchhike. We'd be tempted and spend the dime instead of the nickel. So we'd watch for this one driver that would let us ride home for free. His name was Arthur Pink. But they can't do anything to him now. He's long gone.

We had a lot of fun in those days. And it never cost us anything. Nobody had anything. It was innocent fun. Going down to the park all day when we were ten or eleven.

Vera: It's a shame that kids today are deprived of a lot of those things. I can remember sitting on that beach all day long and our parents never had to worry.

Joyce: It was a nice time of life. ¤

Emancipation Day visitors congregating near the covered bridge over the weir

EMANCIPATION DAY CELEBRATIONS
THE BIG PICNIC

*I*f you ask Harry Harper about St. Catharines' Black history, he'll emphatically tell you that it isn't the exclusive property of the Black community. "Who do you think owned the farms that sheltered my ancestors entering Canada on the underground railway?" he asks, waiting for you to click into his way of thinking. "And it wasn't as if they could just catch a Greyhound bus across the border," he adds with a chuckle.

Harry, who was born in 1925, grew up in a St. Catharines community around Geneva Street and Welland Avenue. One of his neighbours and boyhood chums was Joe McCaffery, a former Mayor of St. Catharines. During his term as Mayor, Joe was a frequent visitor and a proud supporter of the British Methodist Episcopal (BME) Church, of which Harry is one of the leading members. Black history in St. Catharines is centered in the BME Church. Built on land purchased in 1840, the site is situated at the end of the underground railway, around the corner from where the legendary Harriet Tubman rented a boarding house and helped integrate runaway slaves into free society.

The Harper family was one of many families to settle in St. Catharines, arriving in 1824 from South Carolina. Included in the list of persons finding freedom across the Niagara River is Rev. Josiah Henson, whom many believe was the model for the Harriet Beecher Stowe's abolitionist novel, Uncle Tom's Cabin. A former Church's minister, the Rev. Wm. McHenry Vintes, went on to baptize Billy Graham in 1922, and Dr. Ralph Bell, a former church member, is a present day close colleague of Graham.

The name Bertrand Spencer Pitt has special significance to St. Catharines. A follower of Marcus Garvey, the Black nationalist who founded the Universal Negro Improvement Association (UNIA), Pitt held the post of president of the Toronto Chapter early this century. It was Pitt who was the moving force behind establishing the famous and well attended Emancipation Day Picnics at Lakeside Park beginning in the 1920s.

On August 1, 1834, an Act of Imperial Parliament took effect throughout the British Empire to allow for the gradual emancipation of the nearly 800,000 people of African descent held in bondage under the British flag. Emancipation Day celebrations began in St. Catharines as early as 1835. Later on, under the auspices of UNIA, Lakeside Park was chosen as the site for the 'Big Picnic' due to its accessibility to people on both sides of the border and to the existence of Lake Ontario steamers which could bring people from Toronto. The picnics reached their zenith with an estimated attendance of 6000 to 8000 people, until factors such as Spencer Pitt's retirement and the end to steamer travel caused its decline. The last UNIA sponsored 'Big Picnic' was held in 1951. Today, through the efforts of the Black Community, and especially the work of Ruth Harper a few hundred or so people gather in early August at Lakeside Park to celebrate Emancipation Day.

'Butterfly' dresses were the fashion.

HARRY, RUTH & JIM HARPER,
MARJORIE DAWSON:

"We were about eight or nine when we first began attending the picnics," Jim says. All agree except Marjorie who insists she was a teenager. The mid-thirties seems to be a time period they can agree on.

"Lots of Americans would come, but I think most of the people were Canadian," Marjorie claims. "They'd come from Toronto on the boat starting as early as 9:00 a.m. That was a great excitement, that boat coming in. Everybody was there to meet that boat. You know we'd have relatives coming that we hadn't seen for years.

Harry shares some insights. "At that time about 90% of the cars were the ones that came from the U.S. because people from here came by streetcar and the rest from Toronto came by boat. The cars were those big touring cars. They were big long things and when they piled out, you thought it was a small city. They had huge trunks and running boards where they had picnic baskets tied on."

Marjorie recalls the trolley ride. "It was something going to Port Dalhousie on that trolley ride. I always thought it was going to break going over that trestle. When you looked down all you could see was water.

When asked what it was like from the point of view of a child in those days, Ruth answers—"Fascinating! What fascinated me was the dancing. My mother had nine kids so we didn't have a lot of money and couldn't go in the dance hall. But I used to watch them. And then there were the rides and the games and the barbecue—I loved the smell of that barbecue."

"The part that always sticks with me," Jim says, "is when we were about 13 or 14 and getting interested in girls. Every time we'd meet a good looking girl we'd try to shine up to her, and just when you got to the part of when you were holding hands someone would come up and say 'don't you know who that is? That's your cousin so and so . . .' There's an hour and a half work shot to bits! So you start all over, and . . . another cousin!"

Jim recalls the dance hall being close to the pier and the beach with an ice cream stand next to it. "Bruce Anthony had a six piece band there." "And Willie Wright from Toronto" Marjorie adds.

"The music was really lively," Harry says. "That was in the evening and it was mostly attended by teenagers and young adults. By then, if you had young kids, they'd be asleep in the car or ready to go home. But all ages came to the picnic. If they could move they'd get there. You'd see babies and then you'd see really old people clapping to the music. I guess they were reliving their past."

"And another feature," Marjorie says, "is that people dressed up. They bought new clothes. We used to look forward to that—new laces and butterfly skirts. Everybody wanted to look their best."

"And Zoot Suits," Harry says, "Everybody was trying to dress like Cab Calloway. Uncle Harry, he was the money man. I think he saved up from one picnic to the next to give all us guys change. If you got a dollar from him that was like getting a hundred dollars today.

"You can't leave out the fights," Marjorie jibes. "There was occasionally a fight," Harry says. "For the hotels that was a day to really make money, and of course one thing would lead to another. But the police had it pretty much under control. They were always patrolling. The police just about knew everybody. They'd call you by name and you just shook. If you even thought about doing something they'd anticipate it."

The present day picnics don't require a police presence. Apart from being considerably smaller, everyone knows everyone else. "I've been calling it a family picnic," Ruth says, owing to the fact that she promotes the event by mailing flyer invitations to the families that have been part of her extended community over the years. The kids know her as the "Nickel Lady" today, a role that mimics that of her Uncle Harry in years past. Nieces, nephews, grandchildren and others flock to her for tickets and coins to ride the carousel and she makes sure she has a good supply on hand.

The picnic is becoming more and more popular every year and Harry admits they don't know from year to year whether they'll get 200 or 500 attending. Harry Harper's hope is for the Ontario Black History Society (OBHS) to extend its reach to this side of the Lake and take over and expand the annual picnic that he and his family presently organize. ¤

MARTINDALE POND

COLIN JOHNSTON

*F*or those who appreciate nature's beauty at their doorstep, Martindale Pond is a fine shore to live by. The pond, however, was not formed naturally but created as a result of construction of the first lock of the Second Welland Canal in 1845.

Looking past the 'old' Henley Clubhouse

In the past, an interesting though less attractive vista may have been offered due to the flourishing commercial enterprises. Ships, for a time, continued to sail its length toward St. Catharines even after the Welland Canal was relocated, and at one time the shore extended as far as the Maple Leaf Rubber Company factory (Now the Lincoln Fabrics building). The Muir Dry Docks operated in what is now Rennie Park at the north end of the pond up until 1946. In spite of this commercial activity, the pond was used extensively for recreational purposes over and above the predominant sport of rowing. Jim Smiley, the well-loved sharpshooter showman in town, lived on the banks and rented out canoes. He spent many hours on the pond and referred to it as "his local Ganges."

Presently, Martindale Pond is used almost exclusively as a rowing course but occasionally also plays host to canoeists and ice skaters, not to the extent it once did, however. Recently, the creation of parks and wetlands along the shores has added to the natural appeal, and recent improvements have brought the rowing course up to world class standards.

COLIN JOHNSTON

Punt Races

When I was a kid we'd go up the pond to the falls in canoes. That was as far as you could go and you were getting a long way from home. Sometimes we'd swim in the pond, even though we weren't supposed to. None of us ever got sick.

We had punt races on the pond for two or three years. They were little double-ended wooden homemade boats. Whatever lumber we could find, we'd use and we'd plug the holes with tar. I won two races (1932-33). I built the first one myself and my grandfather helped me build the second one. It was made with good lumber and a little fancier than the first one.

I got a better cup with the old one than I did with the new one. The people who owned the King George Theatre, Sullivan & MacIllwaine, got word of us lads with the punts down on the Henley course and they put up a cup. It was a beautiful cup. Chief Smiley helped to organize it. On Saturday afternoon, between Henley races, we lined up and rowed from Smiley's dock down in front of the grandstand. In those days the grandstand was full of people. They hollered and cheered as much for the punt races as they did for the Heavy Eight race. It was great to hear all those people cheering for you. After a couple of years nobody sponsored it and it died.

Tragedy on the Pond

As kids, we used to skate on the pond. There was one thing we did that was against all health rules and regulations. We'd cut a hole in that ice with the back end of our skate and be so darn thirsty that we'd drink that water. Never caught a thing, but, my mother would have shot me, I think.

In the late 1920s, there were two girls, Cecelia Howe and Kathleen Baker, that fell through the ice in the back of McMahon farm. That was a bad spot. The ice back there was always thin; whether the water ran faster through there, I'm not sure.

My grandson saved a couple of kids from drowning a few years back. They went through the ice. He rushed up, got a ladder or something and pushed it out to get these people out of the ice. I believe he got a citation from the City.

It's usually strangers or out-of-towners that drowned. The locals know what's there, how to handle it, and don't take chances. You wouldn't go across from here to the other side in the wintertime unless you've had really severe weather. I wouldn't trust it. I was always a chicken when it came to that ice. There would be half a dozen kids down there in the wintertime and it looked very inviting. I'd sit on Smiley's wharf while they went out and tested it. If they didn't go through, I was all right.

Ice Boating

When I was a little guy, they had ice boats out there just for sport. They had races, but it was short-lived. They were homemade affairs with skates; three skates and one at the back that they steered with; and a sail on it. I can remember when they were coming about. They would shout, "Heads down. We're coming about." And the boom would swing over top.

The conditions had to be just right. You had to have a winter with lots of ice and wind but no snow. My uncle had one and we'd go out on the weekends. It was 10-15 feet long and the span would be 20 by 10 feet. It was lots of fun. ¤

Spectators watch the regatta from the grandstand and from rented canoes

BIRDGENEAU CANOE LIVERY

MARY PATRICK

Mary Patrick's father, Peter Salem Birdgeneau, born in 1888, operated Birdgeneau Canoe Livery on Martindale Pond below Canal Street for 36 years. In those years canoeing was a popular pastime for visitors to Port Dalhousie.

MARY PATRICK:

My father was born in Lindsay, Ontario on March 6, 1888. He was the eldest son in a family of fifteen children—ten boys and five girls. His father was a ship's carpenter and built the cabin interiors of ships. He also built six houses, which he rented to help keep his large family.

In 1906, at the age of 18, my father came to Port Dalhousie looking for work at the Muir Brothers Dry Dock. His trade was also that of ship's carpenter.

He became a close friend of Jim Smiley and Charles Ansell. He joined the Militia and played hockey and in 1912 married Pearl Lennox, a schoolteacher from Western Hill. How they met was rather interesting. He was playing goal and the puck deflected, went over the boards and hit her on the head.

Charles Ansell worked in the shipyard also. He worked in the office but could neither read nor write. Pearl agreed to teach him on the condition that he would see that 'Pete' always had a job at the shipyard. My father and Pearl had three children, Lenora in 1914, June in 1917 and John in 1922. In 1920, he and Pearl purchased a house at 44 Canal Street for $1,100. She died four years later.

Rowers used the Birdgeneau dock to exchange shells with the next crew

In 1926, my father built a canoe livery on the Muir brothers floating ship repair dock. The dock had not been used since 1867, when they built the permanent dry dock. He had a 99-year lease from the government to operate the canoe livery on that property. It cost $2.00 a year. The dry dock had been moved to the side of the new dry dock. His canoe livery housed 40 canoes, with living quarters for two full time workers—a Mr. Chuck Saunders and another man whom we only knew as "Fatz". It was very busy and they worked full-time. Canoes were rented by the hour and cost 15¢ in the beginning. Eventually it went up to $1.00.

When boats were returned late at night after closing time, there were lockers where they could be stored. The canoes were stacked on top of each other. Coloured lights were strung between posts from the corner of the boathouse to the far end of the dock. It could be very dark out there at night and the lights showed both experienced and inexperienced boaters the way back. If they went over too far they'd go over the falls there at the weirs. When you're out at night on the water, you can't see very far unless there's moonlight. My father also built a small lighthouse that helped guide the boats to safety.

One time, my father came home from work and one of the canoes hadn't come back. So, he took the car and drove up to Martindale, on the QEW. Just as he drove up there he saw these two guys coming up from under the bridge. He got out of the car and said, "Where's my canoe?" They had put their feet through the bottom of it with their big army boots. But, he got it home and repaired it.

We never had a drowning, but we had a close call. Two young boys went too close to the bridge where the water goes over the falls. The kids grabbed a hold of the bridge and some local men who happened to be down there pulled them up. The canoe went under the bridge, over the falls and we never found it or any part of it.

There was a dancing platform that was always full of young people and fiddle music on weekends. My father's brothers were musical and they performed for the eager crowds. It was all very gay and festive. I'm very sorry that I missed all of that!

A boardwalk stretched from one end of the dock to the other, with benches installed for customers to sit on while waiting for canoes to return. At the top of the stairs (leading down to the dock) there was a sign. One side said, 'Pete Birdgeneau Canoe Livery', and on the other side it said, 'Thank you, call again'. We were quite busy in those days.

When the regatta was on, it was wild. The rowers would sometimes come and change shells on our dock. They were short of shells back then and after a race they'd have to get out of their shells. The other rowers would come over by motorboat, get in and then the first set of rowers would be taken back.

One time we were down at the boathouse and one of the ships started up its propellers, causing our tie ropes to lift off the moorings. We went floating. All that was holding us was the electrical wires. I had to run up to the house and have my mother call the shipyard. They turned the boat's propellers off and pushed us back with a tug.

Every spring there was work to do. The canoes had to be sanded by hand and varnished. My dad was forever re-enforcing the bottom of each canoe putting an extra rib between the existing ones. Strips of carpet were placed on the bottom to protect each one from the ladies high heels. Those sharp heels could go right through the bottom when they stepped in! They were each provided with four pillows and a wooden backrest—a pillow to sit on, a pillow for their backs and one for each of their arms. Occasionally when the man preferred to half kneel, he'd want one for under his knee. Also they were given a parasol to keep the sun off their heads, and in the evenings a blanket was provided to ward off the cool winds that came off the water. They were really well taken care of. By 1937, dad had downsized and they didn't give the parasols anymore. I suppose the women didn't care anymore if they got the sun on their heads. Back then, they had no lifejackets. My father would give them a paddling lesson. He'd show them how to properly switch from side to side to paddle by putting it behind your head so they wouldn't get the ladies legs all wet. Anyone under 16 had to have a note from their parents. We had a whole box of them—some of which were forged. My father never threw any of them away.

The Dalhousie and the Northumberland brought picnickers from Toronto daily. Many spent part of the day at Lakeside Park and then came to canoe on the pond. Many would leave just in time to catch the last boat home. My father said that sometimes they would go tearing down the street—just running as fast as they could. Young couples would come and have wiener roasts on Read Island (now Henley Island). Some would paddle up the winding pond, under the trestle and the little bridge at Martindale Road, right up as far as the rapids at Wellandvale. Then they'd come back or paddle to the Island. They also watched the Henley from the side of the course.

In 1937, my father married Miss Irene Vanclieaf (my mother). She was the maid for William Muir and his sister Nettie who lived on Queen Street (now Dalhousie Avenue). He just couldn't get away from the Muirs. They had two children, Peter and me.

A few years later Fatz, one of the helpers, accidentally drowned. My father never got over that. Fatz couldn't swim very well and he fell off the dock. Instead of waiting until he came up, he started swimming under water and he went under the big dock. From that day on, my father was so nervous. As children, when we were down there swimming, we always had to tell him when we went up the stairs to our house on Canal Street. Otherwise, he wouldn't know whether we'd gone up or fallen into the water.

By 1942, Chuck Saunders had decided to retire. All those years after Chuck Saunders left, my mother would run down these 60 stairs and rent the canoes until we got out of school. Then she would send us down. In the evenings, after my father got home from work, he would run it.

By this time my father was general foreman at the dry docks and his health was not good as he had diabetes. He decided to downsize and sold all but 12 of the 40 canoes. He gave two to his long time friend Jim (Chief) Smiley and bought two new ones. My brother claimed one of them and I the other. Chief only had one canoe at the time, so this helped his business grow. Chief gave me a paddle when I was a little girl and I still have it. I remember often my father would go over to the end of the dock and he'd yell, "Jim, got any canoes left?" And, if he did, my father would send the people over, otherwise they'd sit and wait. We were that busy!

My father built a cottage with a rustic fence around it where part of the former building stood. He made a sign from driftwood and called it 'Henley View'. It was rented to tourists and to the rowers from Hamilton Leander Boat Club during regatta week. My father was quite creative.

After a time, the dock at the end where the canoes were kept was beginning to sit low in the water. My dad built a large watertight box and my brother Peter and I watched in awe as he deftly caulked the seams. I couldn't get over how fast he worked with that smelly rosin rope. This was something he had done for years in the shipyard while building barges. It was then lowered into the water and filled. Steel straps were placed across it and anchored in place with steel spikes hammered into the huge timbers of the dock. The water was then pumped out and the buoyancy box brought the dock back up again.

In 1947 my father had a stroke. During the following year, while he was recuperating, he decided to build three kayaks in the basement at 44 Canal Street. He called them KA, KB, and KC. My brother and I helped him put the screws in and he would tighten them. We didn't do it too long, because that was work! The kayaks were a big hit with the customers. He made double paddles by joining two together. They

Peter Birdgeneau on his canoe livery dock below Canal Street

were great fun because then you could go really fast.

My brother Peter and I had a great childhood, catching frogs or at least trying to. Our father caught turtles and painted our initials on them. We fished and went on trips to the island. We searched that Island looking for the place where Chief Smiley supposedly hid out from the authorities but we never found it. We didn't know whether it really happened. My father told us the story, perhaps so we'd go up there and have fun.

In the spring, we went by canoe to get spring leeks on the banks up near General Motors. We'd dig out the leeks, bring them back and have a good feast. Each fall, we would go with our father and look for lost paddles along the shorelines. He would sit and we would paddle. He usually ended up paddling home, as we were too tired. I was seven or eight at the time. We swung on the vines on the island, fell in the water catching frogs and listened to the bullfrogs at night.

Our father told us about the horses pulling the barges along the canal and the days when he was a young lad in Lindsay. He and his brothers used to go into the Scugog River, lie on their backs and get the leeches on themselves. Then they'd go to the doctor's and he'd remove them and give them a penny apiece. They used them years ago for healing purposes. I asked my father, "Didn't that hurt?" "Sure," he said. "But it was worth a penny." Back in those days a penny was worth a lot.

In 1949, the dock was starting to sit too low in the water again. This time the floor was taken up in the boathouse and a big steel tank was placed and anchored. A small one was also placed at the end of the building. They used the same method as before and the dock was back up again. We were well out of the water!

Every spring, for years and years, my dear mother would get on the streetcar (and later the bus) and she would go uptown and get fabric. Then she would re-cover about 60 cushions to be used in the boats. They had to be replaced because they got faded, wet and smelly. The water wasn't that clean down there. She also had to have spares in case some got wet. She'd sit up at the house at 44 Canal Street and my father used to say to her, "It's a good thing you don't drive because you'd be charged with speeding." Her sewing machine would be going that fast.

My dad died of a heart attack in October 1954. Peter was 14 and I was 16. My mother, Peter and I continued to operate the canoe livery along with two young men who came from Cardinal, Ontario. They came up looking for work and rented the cabin on the dock. One of their brothers, D'Arcy Patrick came up and that's whom I married in 1957. My brother married in 1961.

In 1962, my mother Irene decided to sell the canoes. It was getting dangerous for her to be down there in the evenings by herself. She was there alone during the week, but on the weekends we would come and help. Mr. Parkins, who used to live at the top of the stairs, would watch to see that she came up every night. The next year, the firemen asked if we were going to use the buildings anymore. They were worried about kids going down there and drowning. We took out a few mementos and then the buildings were burned. Our mother stood on the banks of the pond with the photographer from the St. Catharines Standard and sadly watched as they towed the dock and what was left of the buildings up to Henley Island. It was still sitting high in the water! Then they piled fill on it and sunk it. It's under the parking lot on Henley Island. The caption under the picture in the Standard read "The end of an era". It truly was a sad day for the Birdgeneau family. My mother died on December 26, 1993, six weeks before her ninetieth birthday. The house on 44 Canal Street was sold in 1995. ¤

The 'old' Henley Clubhouse and boathouse

THE SPORT OF ROWING
CLAUDE SAUNDERS

C *laude Saunders has been a 'Henley Personality' for more than half a century. His career began in 1931 at the age of eighteen and continues to this day. An Olympic rower and an early promoter of women in rowing, his lengthy list of accomplishments includes being the Regatta Chairman for the Royal Canadian Henley Regatta from 1952 to 1997.*

He has been awarded the Order of Canada and elected to the Canadian Sports Hall of Fame. To this day Claude Saunders remains an active and energetic individual. His reflections on the past provide valuable insights into the sport of rowing.

CLAUDE SAUNDERS

A Background Brief

I was 18 when I first started to row. I became involved in rowing in the fall of 1931, rowing for the Leander Boat Club, Hamilton. I rowed with them competitively from 1931 to 1948.

In 1932 I was spare man for the Olympic team that represented Canada. In those days it was club teams that went, but they didn't have sufficient funds for spare men, so I didn't go. Our club went to the Olympic games in Los Angeles and our crew was third, which was the first bronze medal Canada had ever won in rowing. We had beat the English and in those days we were referred to as 'Colonials'.

In 1933-34 I rowed in an eight which won the intermediate and senior race here. In 1936 our club represented Canada in the Olympic games in Germany. In 1939 we won the trials to represent Canada in Helsinki and, of course, they were cancelled due to the War.

Then in 1948 I was rowing a single and I was spare man for the Canadian team that rowed in the Olympic games in London, England. In 1960 I was Manager of the Olympic team in Rome. In 1977-78, I was Manager of the Canadian team that participated in the World Championship Regatta held in New Zealand.

I rowed professionally from the age of 18 to 36. The last time I rowed was in 1987. When I came down here for the Henley it was just a two-day regatta. Over the years, of course, it increased. The number of clubs and competitors grew. Then it became a four day regatta.

One thing is, if you go down to Rennie Park and look up the course, not much has changed since I've been coming down here in 1931. If you look on the left hand side, all the trees are the same. They haven't touched anything.

Henley Island was called Read Island at one time. It was owned by Mrs. Read and later bought by Ted Nelson for $5500 in the late 1950s. The Reads used to go there for family picnics. They had a farmer's market. When her husband died, Ted used to take her out shopping. He talked her into selling it for rowing. That bridge came from the Port Weller Dry Docks. It was something they had down there—parts of old ships or something. The Henley Corporation spent a lot of money a few years ago doing repairs to it.

The weigh-ins used to be done in the Lock Tender's shanty before everything moved to Henley Island. The Island was purchased in 1958 and the bridge was put in the next year.

Women In Rowing

In 1972 women came into rowing. I was all for it but there were various clubs that were against it. And the Argonaut Rowing Club was the last club to give in and let women row for them. I'll tell you a story about that. When women came into rowing we had McMaster University rowing at our club. We had women come down and they wanted to row. I told them that, unfortunately, we only had one shower room and one locker room and we didn't have any facilities for women.

They said, "What if we came down here prepared to row and then left, could you supply us with rowing equipment?"

Well I'm in a corner now! So I said certainly. So the women came down in two vans from the University. And they would come down at night, go out in an eight, row, come back and put the boats away, get in their vans and go back to the University and have their showers.

Today in the Royal Canadian Henley Regatta we have about 2600 competitors and 65% of them are women. I can't believe it!

I talk to our coaches and they would rather coach women because, afterwards, when we are finishing rowing at night, to cool down they run for a mile. The fellas will run for a couple of blocks till the coach can't see them, then they'll walk. The women will run all the way there and all the way back.

Safety And Equipment

There was a tragedy that happened at our club around 1934. It was in a four. Our club was in the middle of Burlington Bay. We had a rule that you don't go down towards the beach because the wind really blows. We had a four that went out and instead of heading up to the western part of the bay, went east and it was a west wind. They got out about half a mile and the boat filled up with water. It was down right opposite the Stelco docks. Two of the fellas decided to stay with the boat and washed up on the beach. Two decided to swim to shore to the Stelco dock which looked quite close. One made it and the other one drowned. Always stay with the boat! From then on we had the

John Joseph Ryan—Turn-of-the-century Henley Regatta champion and grandfather of Charles Ryan, present Henley Regatta Chairman

cooperation of the life saving training by the Red Cross. We had demonstrations. The Canadian Coast Guard has new laws coming out. But where do you put the life jackets? They are quite adamant about this. I think it will be resolved though.

One of the problems with rowing today is that even on a beautiful warm May day the water can be like glass but the temperature is still approximately 38-40 degrees (F). We have a sign that was put up by the Hamilton Harbour Commission: "COLD WATER KILLS". If you are in 38 degree water for ten minutes you are dead.

In rowing they say a wooden boat has more life to it than a plastic boat. At our club there is a difference of opinion. The sailors like a wooden boat. They say it has more life to it. And that's an argument that has been going on for years and years in rowing. One thing I found out was that they might make a dozen boats off the same mold but they'd only get one that is a fast one. And we had one in our club way back in 1934. They had bought it from Simms, an English boat builder. It was a dandy. I'd never seen a boat so fast.

I learned something in 1936. Bob Hunter was our coach and tried to tell the boat builder, a designer, what he wanted. We had that boat built—and it never won a race.

Sportsmanship

I saw, what in my mind was one of the finest displays of sportsmanship on behalf of a female competitor. The University of Massachusetts was here once in the Senior Women's Eight. Jim Dietz, who was a famous sculler, coached them and was a personal friend of mine. They came up here and they won the Senior Women's Eight. About three weeks after that I got a letter from him saying that prior to coming to the Henley, they had had an accident. One girl was so badly injured they put her into the hospital. They had to put a spare in. The spare girl came up and rowed and on the way home from the Henley, stopped into the hospital where the girl was and gave her her medal. The coach wrote me later and I got in touch with the medal manufacturer and he supplied a medal to replace it. I got a nice letter of thanks back.

Rowing in an eight—there is something magic about it. It's eight men in a boat and all they have to do is the same thing at the same time. That's the trick. It's on and on. You've got an eight with eight different personalities in it. It doesn't take you long, when rowing in the boat, to realize that if you're going to make the boat go fast, you've all got to do the same thing together at the same time. Now isn't that a lesson in life?

I've gone through life and there's been a lot of people I worked for that I disliked, but I knew if I wanted to make a success of what we were doing, we all had to work together.

I've rowed in all the boats and rowing in a single is lonely. I got more fun out of rowing in an eight. You will have a clash of personalities, but all must work together as a team.

Henley Personalities

There was a fella by the name of Bill Thoburn (1905-1997). Bill was a policeman for a while and then he was a professional gambler in those kind of poker games that moved around in the city. He got out of the police force and made himself a mint of money. He used to run the Labatt's games at the old Legion after the regatta. That was where all the big crap games were. He'd take all the bets in the grandstand—crews against crews. In those days the top four to five rows of the grandstand would be full of cameras. I can still see Bill with the money between his fingers.

They used to gamble at night. The races used to finish around six o'clock and the crews would go out training. The gamblers would be watching the crews to see who was the best. There's none of that today to my knowledge but it was a big thing then. If you read about the history of rowing back in Ned Hanlan's days, gambling was a big part of it from the 1930s to 1950s. It stopped in the early 1950s.

Ned Hanlan was a rumrunner from Toronto Island. He kept in training by beating the police who were trying to catch him. It was illegal but it wasn't enforced.¤

Chief Smiley, well, he was a character. In those days during Henley they'd float a big platform out there. It must have been around 30 to 40 feet square. Chief used to come out there all dressed up and put on a shooting demonstration and performance in front of the grandstand. He never rowed but he had a rowing shell named after him. ¤

An aerial view of the rowing course during lowered water levels c.1940

JAMES J. 'CHIEF' SMILEY
(1885–1948)
A LOCAL LEGEND

*M*arch 18th *marks the anniversary of the death of a man who has become a Port Dalhousie legend. James 'Chief' Smiley lived his life in a unique and non-conformist style; hence, it was only fitting that his death, though tragic, be equally unconventional and spiced with drama, spectacle and irony.*

Born on September 20, 1885, in Port Dalhousie where his father operated a boat works, Jim grew up along the banks of the Twelve Mile Creek, a playground which he later came to refer to as "his local Ganges." There is no doubt about his love for his town that offered him a lifestyle to suit his demeanor. Having gained a bit of fame and notoriety as a 'sharpshooter' on the vaudeville circuit during the early part of the century, he returned and settled in his home town to a life of leisure and recreational pursuit.

Stories about Chief abound. Most are anecdotes retold by the older members of the community—the particulars of which vary from person to person. Such is the nature of legends.

The Smiley family lived in a house on Queen Street (Dalhousie Avenue) behind where McArthur School once stood (now condominiums). Jim lived there when he was a boy. He worked as a barber in Charles Rutherford's shop (below Canal St.) early on, and

there is a reference to him earning money in the morning so he could buy ammunition and canoe up to Read (Henley) Island with his partner, Miss Hutton, for some target practice. There is also a tale of him shooting the heel off the shoe of a man in his barbershop.

Though it appears that he was well liked and respected by the townsfolk, a story in the July 16, 1903 issue of The St. Catharines Standard documents one of his escapades at nineteen years of age which did bring embarrassment upon his 'eminently respectable' family. Depending on which version you may read or hear, he either instigated or was enticed into stealing a pair of rubber boots from the Maple Leaf Rubber Factory (Lincoln Fabrics). The article claims that, in his escape, he fired a shot at the constable on duty. It is assumed that, following this incident and after recovering from a broken pelvis incurred in his flight, he and Miss Hutton left for their vaudeville tour.

Sponsored by both the Winchester and Remington ammunition companies, they traveled throughout the continent billed as Smiley and Hutton on billboard marquees. During this time he may have married and did in fact father a son, though neither returned to Port Dalhousie with him. It appears Jim Smiley was back in town during the start of W.W.I where it is said he hid out on Read Island (sometimes dressed as a woman, as some stories claim) in order to evade conscription. A common belief is that he wasn't avoiding duty but rather wanted to be paid for his services teaching men how to shoot with skill, and ultimately he did go to England to do just that.

After the war, he returned to Port Dalhousie where he lived out his life as a well known and well-respected, though somewhat eccentric, character about town. His sister owned a house at the end of Ann Street overlooking Martindale Pond where he lived until the house was sold in 1925. At this time he moved into a one-room dwelling built above a boathouse on the pond bank (at Ann Street) where he earned a meager living renting out canoes.

In about 1920 he was made custodian of the St. Catharines Rowing Club taking care of their newly constructed shell house. On occasion he was hired to train police officers how to shoot, was a police constable in Port Dalhousie briefly, and even fulfilled the role of

Acting Chief of Police in Port Dalhousie during the Police Chief's illness.

Charles Rutherford's daughter, Port Dalhousie resident Margaret Steele, recalls a story told by her father: "Chief acted as a police constable on busy weekends in Port. One weekend, Chief decided to re-route traffic bound for Lakeside Park, off Front Street (now Lakeport Rd.) and up Lock Street. The butcher on Front Street, who also operated a gas pump, considered this to be a personal affront due to a long running feud between them." (Former resident, Jack McGrath, claims the dislike for each other began when Chief attempted to resolve a domestic dispute between the butcher and his wife.) "According to the story, the butcher sought Chief out after the traffic re-routing incident and, during a physical encounter, bit off the tip of his thumb."

Chief Smiley, whose name was developed on the vaudeville stage and had nothing to do with his policing duties, was often called upon as a guest speaker at dinners, and was also a regular performer during the Henley Regatta. Between races, a barge would be floated in front of the grandstand, and Chief would entertain the audience with his sharpshooting expertise. The Club eventually, in 1946, dedicated a four person rowing shell naming it the 'Chief Smiley' and it went on to win its championship that year.

There is little evidence to support the idea that Jim Smiley ever wanted a regular job. In fact the evidence is to the contrary. A self-educated and well-read man, he could quote the Bible, the Koran, Shakespeare, Tennyson and others, as well as recite the Rubaiyat of Omar Khayyam. Happy and content living in his one room abode, he led an uncomplicated life accompanied by his books, his guns, a canoe, wine and kids who would regularly come visit him.

Though parents might not have considered him the ideal role model, he was loved and admired by all the young boys in town. Movies were popularizing the wild-west cowboy and, if anything, Chief Smiley certainly portrayed himself as the authentic stereotype.

One story that's often told is of a time when a horse broke its leg in the train tracks running down Main Street and had to be put down.

Someone sent for Chief Smiley to do the deed and, as the news got out, his army of young fans began to gather. But Chief wasn't one to take on such serious business without the application of rouge and powder and attiring himself in his western regalia. Unfortunately, by the time he arrived with a troop of young boys following close behind, the horse had already been dispatched by a local constable—a person who, as the story goes, suffered all the verbal wrath that Chief could effectively deliver upon him.

Another amusing story is told by a man who, as a boy, lived in a house above the bank from Chief's place. Chief used to make toy boats out of wood with a clockwork mechanism to power them. Each boy would have his own boat with his name painted on it and was allowed to come down and sail it between the two piers at any time. All Chief asked for in return for letting them have their fun was that they bring him something. One kid would bring a few lumps of coal, another might bring onions, and someone else might be assigned carrots or an egg. The narrator of this story, who wishes to remain anonymous, was supposed to bring potatoes, and he claims that the trick was to not take so many at any one time that his mother might notice them disappearing. Well one day she caught him heading down the bank with a few potatoes and realized what Chief was up to. Needless to say, this clever shenanigan was brought to a quick close.

Though there were many who loved and admired Jim Smiley, there were those who scorned his lifestyle, which to many may have seemed indolent, self-indulgent and even irresponsible. But the one certainty is that Chief chose it willingly, did not begrudge anyone for having more material wealth than he, did not judge his fellow man, and would not be judged by any other than his God.

As far as being a good role model for young boys, he did express wit, ingenuity and self-reliance. He also exemplified skill and perfection resulting from self-discipline and hours upon hours of practice. But if there is one thing that Chief Smiley did demonstrate above all else, it was how to be happy in the absence of material possessions.

It would appear that James Smiley was happy through life right up to the night of his death. His life ended in the wee hours of the morning of March 18, 1948 with an ironic twist. Irish by blood and merry by nature, he had been in downtown St. Catharines celebrating St. Patrick's Day and returned home by streetcar late in the night. No one is sure how his home caught fire, though speculation blames the wood stove. The wood frame building, which contained numerous books as well as ammunition, burned like a box of matches. According to one eyewitness who, as a young girl, watched from the far shore of Martindale Pond, "It was like the Fourth of July." American reference forgiven, the display resulting from all the bullets and gunpowder blowing up, must have been spectacular. Unfortunately, the perceived danger of bullets whizzing past kept the firefighters at bay and thwarted the rescue of Chief who was found lying just a grasp away from the outside door, not at all burned but dead from a lack of oxygen.

St. John's Church was full for his funeral and he was interred in St. Andrew's Cemetery according to the obituary, however, no marker for his grave is visible. All that remains to remind us of this Port Dalhousie legend is the stories that people tell. ¤

Chief as a young man canoeing with 'Babe'

CHIEF SMILEY REMEMBERED
RHODA ABEL, JACK KELLAR, NELLIE HARE

*T*he following conversations were recorded in 1977-78.
*The narrators have since passed away but have provided
us with amusing and insightful recollections on Port Dalhousie's most
colourful character.*

*Mrs. Rhoda Abel was a close friend of Chief Smiley, who shared a
special kinship with him and, occasionally, the stage holding his
targets. Jack Kellar was one of the many young boys who found a
local hero to look up to and, in time, gained a valuable friend. Mrs.
Nellie Hare spoke warmly and with admiration for her dear friend, and
touchingly recounts the circumstances of his death.*

RHODA ABEL:

I was always friendly with James Smiley and he chummed with my
brothers. Of course when my mother went to board with Mrs. Smiley
he was not born yet, so I feel our friendship started before either of us
was born. Jimmy was five maybe six years older than me. He looked
very young and kept himself well. A very active and smart man!
Jimmy Smiley was not a nut. Some people thought he was a fool and
crazy but he was a clever boy, very clever. But he never went to
school much. He used to play hooky all the time. He was one of the
best self-educated men in this town. He was so interesting and I
enjoyed talking to him. Listen, you couldn't mention a book that he
couldn't tell you who wrote it and everything in it—the Bible, the
Koran. He received his education from books and could quote from
plays, poetry and history. Oh, he surprised the literary club. They
asked him to speak once and when he was through one of the ladies
said, "I can't understand why you live down there in that old shack
when you are so knowledgeable." "Why I don't live there," he said. "I

just eat and sleep there. I live in my books. When I get bored I take a trip up the Nile and visit Cleopatra, or I go down the Ganges and watch the people beating on the walls of China."

Of course he carried Omar Khayyam's Rubaiyat around with him wherever he went. He, like me, knew it all by heart. He thought a lot of this gentleman. Omar Khayyam was a great wine drinker. It seems all he did was drink wine and try to find out what was going to happen after he was gone.

With a revolver he'd cut thread from a needle and puncture silver balls and pennies in the air. Sharp eye to do that. I used to hold shots for him on the stage. He'd shoot things off my head and buttons off my coat. He wanted me to go on professionally with him in St. Catharines but I wouldn't. But if the Church was having a show, I always held his targets. Anybody who knows me knows that I was never afraid of Jimmy Smiley. I was afraid of me. I knew he was perfect and wasn't going to shoot me. You know what you can't do is close yours eyes because then you move. When he'd shoot the buttons off my coat he'd turn his back to me, look into a mirror and shoot over his shoulder. Zip, zip, zip. Five buttons. I remember one time I was standing on a box to get a little higher while he was shooting over his shoulder. I heard him shoot five times. 1-2-3-4-5. As I knew he hardly ever missed I went to step down. The audience screamed, "No!" He knew. He held back the gun. I said, "Oh, you missed one." And so I stepped back up and let him shoot.

Everyone knew he was a perfect shot and he often assisted the police on their manhunts. If they were looking for someone with a gun, a murderer, or robber, they'd come for Jimmy. There were no regional police then and the Ontario Police paid him for his efforts.

Once he got on the aerial swings in the park. I'll never forget this. Somebody on the swings was throwing targets up for him and he missed a couple of them. When he got off he said, "Well I missed a couple that time but I want you people to know my ancestors were not flies."

He met Buffalo Bill Cody on the circuit but was never in his show. He loved and admired Buffalo Bill and it was one of the greatest things in his life when they met.

JACK KELLAR:

Chief was a barber in his early days and he had a shop on Front Street next to Blair's who ran the Walkerly. He would do shaves because that's where the money was. At that time it was 10 cents for a shave and 15 cents for a haircut. A shave was faster and he could make 10 cents in half the time it would take to cut hair. Saturday night was a busy night and he stayed open until 11 o'clock. The men would come in for a shave on their way uptown. If they got a shave late Saturday night, they could go to church Sunday morning without having to shave.

Chief Smiley—happy in his modest home

The story is told that one day one of the fellows in the shop was annoying the Chief by putting his feet on the rungs of the chair, leaning back and then letting the chair come down with a bang. He was shaving someone and he'd jump every time. "You're going to keep up until I'm going to fix you," he said. But the fellow kept on. So, he turned and in a flash grabbed his gun from the shelf and shot the heel off the man's shoe.

Chief told me that when he was young he would buy maybe 500 rounds of ammunition, go up to Read Island and wouldn't come home till it was all gone. He said he spent hours and hours practicing. That's how he learned to shoot.

Chief went on that vaudeville tour. He started out in the Old Griffin Theatre in St. Catharines. Mr. Griffin used to have a string of theatres throughout Canada and the United States. He would hire actors and act as their agent. Chief went on the vaudeville tour with him.

He had a Winchester and a Remington, and for a percentage he represented those companies on his vaudeville circuit. When he got up to shoot he'd say, "Now I'm going to do this shot with a Remington rifle and I'm also going to use Remington ammunition, which is very good ammunition. I use nothing else but Remington ammunition in a Remington rifle." Then he'd do a few shots, lay down that rifle and pick up the other and he'd say, "This is a Winchester rifle. It's a very fine rifle, and I use exclusively Winchester ammunition because that's the only ammunition I'd touch."

March 18, 1948—the aftermath of the fire that took his life

An old friend of Chief Smiley, who wishes to remain anonymous, tells a story that happened in 1903 when Jim Smiley was 19 years old.

For awhile the (Maple Leaf) Rubber Factory was losing a lot of shoes and they couldn't find out where they were going. So they hired a private detective agency and they sent one of their crack operators over. He boarded with the Smiley's. The detective got a job in the factory and they shifted him all around so that he could take a look at things. Still the shoes were being stolen. You see, meantime the factory was complaining to the detective agency that their agent was no damn good and wasn't getting any place. He'd been in Port for quite awhile. So he said to Chief how easy it would be. "All I have to do when I'm working there tonight is to unlock a window and pass the stuff out the window. You come across in your canoe and tie up to the wharf." Well he fell for it. He paddled across the canal and got in through the window that was left unlocked. Then he said to Chief, "Pick up those rubber boots there, they look like a size that would fit you." So Chief picked them up, and the fella said, "I'm a private detective. You're under arrest." Well naturally Chief dropped the boots and he ran from the window and jumped out. They'd built a wooden platform down there where the boats used to tie up to load shoes bound for Kingston and Montreal. Well when Chief jumped, he intended to clear that loading platform and land in the canal, get in his canoe and paddle home. You know how sophisticated Chief was. He was just going to go home. It never occurred to him that they'd just follow him. He didn't make it though. He misjudged the thing, landed on the wharf and broke both his legs. Well, he crawled over to the canoe, paddled over to the bank, and crawled up. He went from the top of that bank on Ann Street, crawled across the street, through the public school and into his own home. They had a fellow there, a sort of Justice of Peace. Chief told me they had the court case in his bedroom because he had two broken legs.

They sentenced him to three months. He had nothing to do with the original lost shoes; he was just a fall guy. They didn't want to send him to the clink because he had two broken legs. But when he could walk he would have to serve his sentence. So I don't think he ever enjoyed himself so much in all his life because he became a public hero. The private eye had to get out of town or they'd have tarred and feathered him. Chief spent his three months in the old jail on Niagara Street. That's torn down. Every Sunday afternoon that was the thing to do, go up and see Chief Smiley. People would take him boxes of chocolates, cigarettes, and magazines. He lived the life of Riley.

NELLIE HARE:

Don't try to tell me anything about Jimmy because he was a good scout and a complete gentleman at all times. Some thought otherwise. Jealousy, you know. But he was really and truly good.

He was as smart as a whip and well trained in everything. Nobody could equal him. He could go through the Bible with you or give you the Classics. He was nobody's fool. He'd come to my house any old day and we'd sit up on the stoop and talk and laugh for hours. "Nellie, I'm just as crazy as the fox," he'd say. And he was right too. He'd be saying something to me and then he'd start to swear. Hell was a lovely word for him to say. "Oh hell Nellie, you don't believe a thing I say." And of course I'd laugh and say, "No, I don't."

Being an expert on Winchesters, he trained the police up in St. Catharines. He had his regular belt on with his guns at his side, his ten-gallon hat, and his boots were the prettiest things you ever laid your eyes on. Oh he was a clever man and fooled the public for years during the first part of the war (W.W. I). They were conscripting all the boys and, of course, he was able. He said he'd go to England to train them if he were given a title. They wanted him to live on $1.25 a day and he knew he was worth more than that because he made more teaching guns. He wouldn't even allow them to see him. He'd duck over to the island, and as he knew every knoll and crevice, they were unable to find him. When they gave in to him he began training the men. (He was a sniper in W.W. I and there were very few then.)

He wanted to teach me to shoot but I refused. I only handled the gun once and was frightened of it. But with him it was just like taking a drink of water.

Many people vividly remember the night he died. It's felt that he went out in a blaze of glory—the way he lived.

Nellie Hare: He'd been up in St. Catharines with some friends celebrating the 17th of March, St. Patrick's Day. He caught the last bus and said he was going home to light his fire. He was always a nighthawk. When he got home, he must have lit his fire because it was cold. Instead of it burning as it should have, it got out of control. Nobody ever really knew for sure. When the siren went, my husband, who was a volunteer fireman, took the truck around and hollered to me. "Don't come! It's Jimmy's place!" And of course I started to shake. To think that my husband, who was his friend for years, had to open the door and get him. The flames were shooting up so high and they couldn't save him. He almost got out, you know. His place had two doors, and he was found between them. As the smoke was so great, he couldn't reach the latch. There was nothing the firemen could do. You see, he had a lot of ammunition and they were afraid to have anyone go near as the bullets were exploding with the heat.

There was not another character in the history of Port Dalhousie who could compare with Chief James Smiley. His familiar figure, sometimes dressed in western clothing and high-heeled boots, and at other times in blue blazer, white pants and sneakers, was greatly missed by many. As well as being a learned man, an excellent marksman, and proficient with the bullwhip, he was also a skillful canoeist. He helped chart the rowing course, assisted in the annual preparation for the Henley Regatta, and entertained the crowds with his sharpshooting skills.

Those fortunate enough to have known James Smiley have kept his memory alive by recounting tales of his prowess, ingenuity, versatility and innocent chicanery. It was a sad day when he died. The fire, which took his life, also destroyed everything he owned including his fine collection of books. To this day there is some question as to the fate of his rifle and pearl handled guns. Strangely enough, they were never found in the debris. ¤

The Midway c.1955

*The Restaurant at the east
end of the beach in
Lakeside Park c.1941*

*A streetcar leaving
Lakeside Park c.1905*

The original carousel building

The unique carousel lion

CONCLUSIONS

*T*he photograph we chose for our front cover was found among the many Christine and I collected over the past twenty-odd years. We have no idea where it came from, who gave it to us, or who the girls are? We'd like to think that someone knows and, of course, we'd love to find out. For us, the picture epitomizes our sub-heading *'and the best was free'*.

As Port Dalhousie prepares to enter the next millennium, the community faces new and exciting challenges. Bounded by water, there is a limit to growth, yet people are once again arriving in ever increasing numbers to take advantage of the recreational and entertainment facilities. The best is still free but a healthy community must have an effective economic engine in order to develop. Our engine is undoubtedly the tourism industry—that same force that carried us through the years following the relocation of the Welland Canal and the resulting end to our industrial era.

The 20th century has been witness to remarkable change for Port Dalhousie. From a thriving industrial centre to the most popular beach on the Great Lakes, the human quality has carried us through with fond memories of the past. Even during that short period as a forgotten neighbourhood, those who called 'Pordaloozie' their home maintained the same pride and spirit as had their predecessors. Without it, the old town may never have emerged from the shadows to carry on as the unique, proud and inviting neighbourhood that it is today.

The future is unfolding and Port Dalhousie is evolving. The direction is clearly defined by our collective recollections of the past.

David Serafino

ACKNOWLEDGEMENTS

*I*n the research, organization and writing of a book such as "*A Nickel a Ride*", the magnitude of the project expands with the effort and, subsequently, requires a great deal of support and assistance. If it were not for the people who gave generously of their time to share their inspirational accounts and photographic treasures, it would not have been possible to produce this book.

We realize, as many in our town do, that those who enlighten us of our past are disappearing in our midst. One of the greatest joys in creating this book has been to sit down and interview the unforgettable, vibrant people who gave this project a heart and a soul. We gratefully acknowledge the following three people who have since passed from this world.

Jack Kellar who, as a boy, witnessed the town passing through the prohibition era and was one of Chief Smiley's 'boys'.

Rhoda Abel who, on occasion, performed with Chief Smiley during his sharp-shooting performances.

Nellie Hare, a friend of Chief's who recalls the joy of his life and the tragedy of his death.

Similarly, we wish to express our gratitude to the following:

Colin & Gloria Johnston for recalling those magic moments and defining the personality of the town.

Lawrence Bentz for reflecting on a past that is all but forgotten.

George Graham for his anecdotal story of near tragedy on the Port Dalhousie shore.

Jack Stunt for painting a vivid picture of being young, in a band and on a boat.

Ethel Williamson for eloquently describing a young girl's summers at the beach.

Vera Dudley and *Joyce Dunn* for bringing us back to a time when Lakeside Park was a child's paradise.

The Harper Family—Harry, James & Ruth and *Marjorie Dawson* for their portrait of those significant days of the 'Big Picnic'.

Mary Patrick for an affectionate glance at her father's life on the bank of Martindale Pond.

Claude Saunders for expressing the challenges, achievements and true sportsmanship in the world of rowing.

We also wish to acknowledge those who sent their photographs our way over the past twenty years. Thank you to Agnes Charles, Dennis Cushman, Dan Long, Doug Mackie, Jack McGrath, Gerald Wing, St. Catharines Historical Museum, Centennial Library Special Collections Department, and perhaps a few others.
A very special thank you also goes out to Lana Wainman, for coming up with the title and being supportive and patient throughout this endeavour.

Christine Robertson